The
POWER
of GODLY
WISDOM

The
POWER
of GODLY
WISDOM

Knowing and moving in God's plan

Rob Jones

Sovereign World

Sovereign World Ltd
PO Box 784
Ellel
Lancaster LA1 9DA
United Kingdom

ISBN: 978-1-85240-469-7

Cover design by Terry Dugan Design
Typeset by CRB Associates, Reepham, Norfolk
Printed in Malta

CONTENTS

Other books by Rob Jones:

You Will Receive Power

For more information and to download free Christian resources from the author, visit:

www.receivepower.co.uk

ACKNOWLEDGMENTS

Firstly, I would like to dedicate this book to two lovely Christian ladies, Rose Knight and Julie Almond, who have gone to be with their Lord and Savior, the one they loved so much. Both these ladies knew what it was to love the Lord, and they ministered great encouragement to His people. Both will be deeply missed.

I want to acknowledge and thank Simon Clayton, Eric Normington and especially Rob Matthews for editing and proofreading this book. Your patience and help have been invaluable.

Also, a big thank you to Sovereign Books for taking a risk on an unknown author.

A special thank you to my wife Rebecca, who in so many ways gives up time with me so that the Lord may continue to use me without distractions.

And finally, thanks to the Lord Jesus who in every sense has truly renewed my mind through His wonderful Word and Spirit.

INTRODUCTION

For the foolishness of God is wiser than man's wisdom,
and the weakness of God is stronger than man's strength.
(1 Corinthians 1:25)

There are certain questions we ask during our lives as God's people. For example: "How do I know God's plan for my life?" I have spent many hours listening to Christians who have come to a crossroads in their lives, and are frustrated that God's path did not seem clear to them.

I was in a prayer meeting when a young man declared that he did not have a girlfriend. But surely God wanted him to have a wife! He turned to me in anger and said, "Rob, why does God make it so hard for us to understand His will?" The man's frustration was born not out of rebellion towards God, but a real concern that he could not discover God's plan for his life.

As a response to this and other conversations, I was led back to Scripture to ask: "How does the Bible tell us to discern the wisdom of God's plan for our lives?" The answer amazed me: the Word of God shows us clear pathways for moving in God's wisdom, and living out God's plan in our daily experiences. These pathways release wisdom and discernment into our lives if we follow them.

I learned that when Jesus calls us into relationship with Himself, He works powerfully at the core of our minds, and His power releases godly wisdom into our lives. Following this revelation, I preached a series of sermons on growing in the wisdom of God, which form the basis of the present book.

The book is offered in the belief that as we apply scriptural principles to our lives, the Holy Spirit will take us on a journey of living in a new and powerful way, leading us to the center of God's active wisdom, and unfolding His plan for us. It is a journey of radical obedience that releases anointing into our lives, enables us to reach our full potential, and provides abundant fruitfulness. Discernment is the Father's gift to His children, and the challenge for each of us is to allow God's Word to renew our minds, turning them from the thoughts of this world to the wisdom of God.

Chapter 1

WHY OUR MINDS
NEED RENEWING

Do not conform any longer to the pattern of this world,
but be transformed by the renewing of your mind.
Then you will be able to test and approve what God's will is –
his good, pleasing and perfect will.

(Romans 12:2)

One of the wonderful truths about the work of the Lord Jesus in our lives is that His desire is to take us on a journey of transformation and renewal. He wants to give us a new life, a new beginning through repentance and personal faith in Him.

In John 3:3 we see the reality of a newborn nature: "In reply Jesus declared, 'I tell you the truth, no-one can see the kingdom of God unless he is born again.'" He goes on in verses 6–7: "Flesh gives birth to flesh, but the Spirit gives birth to spirit. You should not be surprised at my saying, 'You must be born again.'"

Through repentance and faith in Jesus' redeeming power, we receive forgiveness from our sins and cleansing from our guilt. We become born again by His Holy Spirit and we receive a new standing, a new relationship with our Father in heaven. The new Father–son relationship with God ends our old lives, and opens up new possibilities for us as His Kingdom people.

Romans chapters 5 and 6 describe this wonderful work of transformation and salvation, found through faith in Christ.

Along with this spiritual transformation Jesus also transforms our minds so that we might live in God's wisdom, working out His plan in our lives. When we give our lives to Jesus we find a transformation of both the spirit and the will. Our will was previously focused on the things of this world, making decisions in line with our own interests and desires. Our will was self-centered, and accountable to no one but ourselves. In fact our will was not free at all, but dominated by the spirit of disobedience at work in the world, resulting in a double-minded life displeasing to God.

In Romans 8:6–8 Paul teaches us:

> The mind of sinful man is death, but the mind controlled by the Spirit is life and peace; the sinful mind is hostile to God. It does not submit to God's law, nor can it do so. Those controlled by the sinful nature cannot please God.

Our will is directly responsible for our decision-making. When my will is focused on me, I will make decisions in line with my intentions. Whatever controls my will controls my life. It may be money, pleasure, family or success, whatever occupies my mind and is central to my desires.

However, when we give our lives to Jesus we accept Him both as Savior and Lord. We bind ourselves to Him by faith, we focus our heart, mind and will on obeying His will and following His purposes for our lives. The resulting freedom that we receive from the things of this world releases us for the will of God. When we know the love of Jesus, the fellowship of the Holy Spirit and the presence of God guiding, comforting and empowering us, our hearts are won over. We submit in loving obedience to His plans. A spiritual throne-room is built in our will, where Jesus is Lord over our lives. This is the sign of a restored mind, centered on Jesus Christ.

I used to live in Nottingham, near a derelict part of the inner city. Old houses had been vandalized, windows smashed, graffiti daubed on the walls, and the whole area was overgrown and wasted. Many complaints were made by the local residents, so the council demolished the houses, flattened the ground, built lovely new houses, and landscaped the surroundings. There was an opening ceremony where the public were allowed to view the changes. Many could not believe the contrast: it all looked so good, fresh and new. The council had taken a rough, damaged area, and renewed it as something useful and good.

This is what God wants to do in our minds! Before we become Christians we make our own decisions, following the habits and morals of the world. We map out plans for our own lives, using our best guesses and hoping that nothing unforeseen will mess it all up. We entertain ourselves in line with our own desires, and as long as it does no obvious harm to others we are content. Ephesians 2:1–3 describes the condition of our lives before finding God's grace and love in Jesus:

> As for you, you were dead in your transgressions and sins, in which you used to live when you followed the ways of this world and of the ruler of the kingdom of the air, the spirit who is now at work in those who are disobedient. *All* of us also lived among them at one time, gratifying the cravings of our sinful nature and following its desires *and thoughts*. Like the rest, we were by nature objects of wrath.
>
> (emphasis added)

As Paul tells us, we have followed the desires of fallen and sinful humanity, our thought processes dominated by the corrupted mentality of the world. However, when we come to the Lord Jesus, Scripture declares that God wants us to build our lives on His unchanging wisdom, to inform the choices we make each day. He wants to transform and renew us in Him.

This renewal of mind enables us to be open to the wisdom of God, and to discern God's plan and direction for our lives. Paul recognized this as part of the walk of a Christian when he wrote in Romans 12:2:

> Do not conform any longer to the pattern of this world, *but* be transformed by the *renewing of your mind*. *Then* you will be able to test and approve what God's will is – his good, pleasing and perfect will.

(emphasis added)

The Greek word used here for "renewing" means "to make new," and its root means "new, fresh, things made new." So in this verse Paul is clearly declaring to Christians that our hearts and minds must be continually set free from the patterns of this world. Then we will be renewed in the plans, thoughts and purposes of God.

If we do not recognize this need for thought renewal from the things of this world, then as Christians we will make wrong choices for our lives. We will bear rotten fruit in our everyday lives. Many of the problems of people I minister to occurred because they made choices in line with the world rather than in line with the Word of God. Jesus is Savior of their lives, but has not become Lord of their will, their desires and their thinking.

Paul recognizes the ability of Christians to be deceived and to allow ungodly thoughts to lead them astray. In 2 Corinthians 11:3 he states: "But I am afraid that just as Eve was deceived by the serpent's cunning, your minds may somehow be led astray from your sincere and pure devotion to Christ." He tells us that the mind is a battlefield that can be affected by many different influences. Right from the beginning of Scripture we see that there are two spiritual kingdoms: God's, and Satan's. The demonic kingdom is allowed by God and has to work under the rules, authority and power that God Himself has established. Therefore the demonic is subject to God, and is allowed to exist only for God's ultimate purpose. The Bible makes it clear that before mankind was made, Satan and a third of the angels in heaven used their free will to rebel against God, and as a result were cast down to earth. Satan allowed the desire to be worshiped into his heart, wanting power and position like God. Likewise, Adam and Eve were tempted and fell into sin. As a result of this Fall, humanity's natural state is to be born spiritually dead, under Satan's control and God's judgment. Sickness, disease, suffering and death have become the norm for all humanity. Physically, spiritually, emotionally, intellectually, sexually – humankind has been affected at every level by the ripple-effect of the Fall in the Garden of Eden.

One of the main battlegrounds of spiritual warfare is the will and thought-life of each individual. In 1 Peter 5:8–9, Peter makes it clear to Christians that the devil is looking for signs of weakness to exploit in our lives:

> Be sober, be vigilant; because your adversary the devil walks about like a roaring lion, seeking whom he may devour. Resist him, steadfast in the faith, knowing that the same sufferings are experienced by your brotherhood in the world.
>
> (NKJV)

By infiltrating the mind, Satan wants to blind the unsaved, and harden them against the Gospel of salvation that Jesus has come to establish. He does this by creating false religions and ideologies that will obscure the truth, and by bombarding people with such busyness and desire for pleasure that they do not have time to explore the important questions of life.

Along with this attack on the minds of the unsaved, Satan also attacks the minds of the saved. He wants to dishonor God by bringing shame and judgment on God's people, tempting a Christian to sin so as to discredit the Gospel of Jesus Christ in the eyes of the unsaved. Typically, Satan targets areas of weakness in our character, subjecting them to temptation and hardship. The name "Satan" means "accuser of God's people," and we will not live in the full victory and freedom of Jesus unless we learn to live a holy and disciplined life before God.

Holiness is the key to defeating the demonic in life. Satan wants to blind people to the truth in Christ and destroy the ability of the Church to witness, because he already stands condemned by God. His demons plant lustful and evil seeds into our imaginations. These thoughts work their way into the human heart and mind, sin is conceived, and sinful action results. Demons feed thoughts into the human mind to intensify the evil that is already there. The aim is to deceive God's people. The process of thought attack goes like this: evil thoughts – lead to free-will choice – which leads to habits of sin – which leads to loss of control – which leads to demonic bondage. Areas where demons tempt us regularly are doubts, temptations, evil thoughts, circles of depression, desire for independence, materialism, pride and fear. Jesus calls Satan the "father of lies"; his desire is to use the minds of individuals to give them a false impression of truth. Thus he gains control of our thought-life. This is why there must be an openness within each of us, to humbly allow the Holy Spirit to teach us God's plan for our lives and our future.

The first step is to recognize that even those of us who have given our hearts to the Lord need our minds renewed. We cannot sow the understanding of the world and expect to reap a spiritual outcome. Galatians 6:7–8 says:

> Do not be deceived: God cannot be mocked. A man reaps what he sows. The one who sows to please his sinful nature, from that nature will reap destruction; the one who sows to please the Spirit, from the Spirit will reap eternal life.

Right now we can decide to develop godly wisdom and understanding for our lives. We can let the Holy Spirit deepen the channels of wisdom in our hearts and minds. We will experience the joy of being disciples of Jesus who bear much fruit, showing ourselves to be His followers.

Scripture gives us a number of different reasons why our minds need renewing in Christ. Firstly, God's way of thinking is not ours. Our decision-making processes have been shaped by our society and the world, including our ideas of reasonable behavior, success, rights and needs. But God thinks and acts according to very different criteria from those of the world. God has a different agenda.

We give our hearts to Jesus and love Him with a passion, but if our minds are not renewed daily we experience conflict between what our hearts say, which are surrendered to Jesus, and what our minds say, which are shaped by the world. Even living by faith becomes difficult, because our rational minds have been shaped by the materialistic mindset of our society. Our minds are influenced by a worldview that comes from fallen society rather than from biblical revelation. Paul makes it clear in Romans 12:2 that the renewing of the mind to transform our daily lives is an ongoing process. If we do not walk down this path, we will not see the blessings and joys of Kingdom living fully manifested in our everyday walk with Jesus. We cannot have one foot in the world and another foot in Christ: this creates double-mindedness, which undermines the trust that we have in Jesus. The result is insecurity, and the failure to live out God's promise in our lives.

Paul teaches us that earthly wisdom comes from the mind of man, but heavenly wisdom comes from God. In 1 Corinthians chapters 1 and 2 Paul compares these two very different forms of wisdom, showing that the wisdom of the world is *not* compatible with the wisdom of the Kingdom. While God's wisdom leads to salvation, freedom, liberty and life, worldly wisdom is empty, self-seeking, proud, and leads to death and decay. It may seem harsh to say these things about the so-called wisdom of worldly man, but ultimately his wisdom is built upon a limited ability to understand the wider picture of creation, now and in the future.

Before we came to Jesus our minds and decision-making processes were shaped by the wisdom and understanding of the world. We took on its ideas, allowing its wisdom to inform our choices and decisions. We allowed its science to tell us what is true about our world, even though many of its greatest theories cannot be proven. By faith we accepted the world's mindset, believing that in it we had found true wisdom, fairness and goodness. Scripture warns us that we must not be deceived by the wisdom of this world, or by the pride that goes with it: for worldly wisdom can become a stumbling block to receiving God's wisdom, which can set us free.

Many who see themselves as wise in the ideas of this world have a problem accepting the simple truths of the Kingdom of God. I have spent many hours with people who have taken time to explore the ancient religions of the world. They have embraced the belief systems and practiced the spiritual disciplines that these religions offer and yet have found no lasting peace, no joy, no salvation for their lives. They have then come to me and been baffled by the simple message of the cross. For many of them the simple wisdom of the cross has been blocked from their minds, so they have not received new life.

In 1 Corinthians 3:18–20, Paul gives us a clear warning about the pride of worldly knowledge:

> Do not deceive yourselves. If any one of you thinks he is wise by the standards of this age, he should become a "fool" so that he may become wise. For the wisdom of this world is foolishness in God's sight. As it is written: "He catches the wise in their craftiness"; and again, "The Lord knows that the thoughts of the wise are futile."

Paul declares that the cross is indeed a stumbling block to those who think they are wise in spiritual or worldly terms. 1 Corinthians 1:22–24 testifies to this:

> For Jews request a sign, and Greeks seek after wisdom; but we preach Christ crucified, to the Jews a stumbling block and to the Greeks foolishness, but to those who are called, both Jews and Greeks, Christ the power of God and the wisdom of God.
> (NKJV)

Yet when we come to Jesus and accept a wisdom that comes from the Lord, we see that what we believed about many things is wrong, and we have built our lives on the sandy foundation of human pride. Through faith in Jesus we have accepted wisdom from God, and we must learn to walk in the fullness of this truth. We must allow the Holy Spirit and the Word of God to transform our minds, so that we may be led by the precepts of God.

The earthly wisdom that we rely on is the foolishness of a simple creature contrasted with the all-powerful, all-knowing, all-present creator God. This passage in 1 Corinthians 1 compares these two wisdoms:

> "I will destroy the wisdom of the wise;
> the intelligence of the intelligent I will frustrate."
>
> . . . Has not God made foolish the wisdom of this world? . . .
> For the foolishness of God is wiser than man's wisdom, and
> the weakness of God is stronger than man's strength.
>
> (verses 19–20, 25)

If we give our hearts to the Lord, but do not renew our minds, we miss the wisdom of God for our lives and families. Even as Christians we can end up building our lives on the limited and foolish knowledge of this world. Not just in salvation knowledge, but also in daily living, the world's thoughts are not the Lord's thoughts. Isaiah 55:8–9 reveals this clearly:

> "For my thoughts are not your thoughts,
> neither are your ways my ways,"
> declares the LORD.
> "As the heavens are higher than the earth,
> so are my ways higher than your ways
> and my thoughts than your thoughts."

The great joy in all this is that through faith in Jesus, God enables us to grow in His wise plans for our lives. However, we first need to understand that His ways are greater than our ways: His thoughts are not the same as the thoughts of our world.

To cultivate dynamic wisdom in our lives, we must allow His Holy Spirit to reprogram our minds from the wisdom of this world, and teach us the purposes that God has for us. The wisdom He wants to cultivate in our lives brings life and freedom. Joy and peace are released as we daily live out the precepts of the Lord. Psalm 19:7–8 tells us:

> The law of the LORD is perfect,
>   reviving the soul.
> The statutes of the LORD are trustworthy,
>   making wise the simple.
> The precepts of the LORD are right,
>   giving joy to the heart.
> The commands of the LORD are radiant,
>   giving light to the eyes.

A second reason our minds need renewing in God's wisdom is to help us live a moral life before God. Having a mind renewed in the Lord is not only about knowing the plans of God and obeying His will; it is also about living a life that is holy and worthy of Him. Galatians 5:16–23 makes it clear that the sinful nature of the unsaved has taken hold of their morals and behavior. So although the lost have a conscience, it is corrupted by the sinful desires of the society we live in. Their nature is bound by a spirit of disobedience. Even as Christians set free from our sinful nature, we need to allow the Word of God to deepen our moral transformation – a change that we have been freed in Jesus to manifest. Otherwise, our minds may lead us into sinful compromise.

Even in the church we find some whose minds are not renewed in the Lord, who rewrite Scripture to justify sinful behavior in our society that the Lord sees as an abomination. With so much of our society soaked in corrupted morality, and so much of our media bombarding our minds with sensual images, it is impossible to live a life pleasing to God *unless* we co-operate with the Holy Spirit in renewing our minds. As Galatians 5:17 says:

> For the flesh lusts against the Spirit, and the Spirit against the flesh; and these are *contrary* to one another, so that you do not do the things that you wish.
>
> (NKJV, emphasis added)

Our blessing as children of God means living lives worthy of Jesus. Our understanding of right and wrong has been shaped by our society. That is why so much sin dwells in the camp of God's people. I have pastored Christians caught up in the sins of the world: drunkenness, sex before marriage, greed, hate and unforgiveness. The Word declares we should no longer conform to the patterns of this world. To live lives with the holiness and purity of Jesus, we need to allow the Holy Spirit to deepen our understanding of God, to open our minds to His renewing processes, so that our behavior comes into line with His holiness.

This is not about our personal freedom or preferences. It is about the precepts that God has laid down on His people to deepen their relationship with Him. If He would not look upon His own sinless Son who carried the sins of the whole world upon His body, then how much more will He not look upon us if we continue in hardened sin? As God's people we do not have the luxury of taking our morals from the world or those around us. We cannot decide what is right or wrong based on what others tell in the world. "Well, they do it!" does not hold up well before a holy God who calls His people to holiness. The moral center of our minds must be submitted to God, and we must allow Him to write His laws on our hearts and minds. This helps us take our eyes off right and wrong as seen by the world, and to understand right and wrong from the perspective of a holy God.

A third reason for minds renewed in the Lord is to enjoy the fullness of what He wants to do in and through us. I have met many Christians who had difficulty understanding who they are in the Lord Jesus. They lacked confidence, joy and security in themselves, even as new creations, because they defined themselves through the eyes of other people rather than through the eyes of God. Many people gain their understanding of who and what they are, their strengths and weaknesses, from families and friends – even when these people have been unkind to them. There are many in our churches who need to come to a biblical understanding of who they are in Christ. There are many who need their minds renewing and setting free, to understand what the Lord says concerning their new identity and their relationship with Him.

The focus of a living faith is Jesus, through all that He has done for us on the cross. As we understand God's purposes, the work of Jesus upon that cross, the new relationship that we have with the Father through faith in the Son, we see ourselves as the Lord sees us. Yes, we are sinners who have rebelled against the Lord and lived our lives for self. But now we are included in Christ we have become saints, children of the Living God. We have been forgiven and cleansed through the precious blood of the Lamb. We have become co-heirs with Christ to the Kingdom of Heaven. As children of God, filled with the Holy Spirit, we understand the lies of evil people that have bound us to a false understanding of who we are.

Whatever people have said about us we are not thick, or ugly, or failures: in Christ, the Lord sees us as His precious children, chosen, called, loved and able to do great things through Christ who strengthens us. Far from our past holding us back, it becomes a springboard that releases us into a powerful understanding of who we are, shaped and defined by the Lord Himself. Our realization of who we are is mediated into our lives by the One who saw us knitted together in our mother's womb, the One who knows the words on our lips before we utter any of them, and the One who knows our motives and our thoughts even before we act one of them out. I tell many people in the church: *In the Lord Jesus Christ, your past does not have to be your future.* For when you see yourself through the eyes of God, all things become new and full of hope. As Romans 8:28–30 says:

> And we know that in all things God works for the good of those who love him, who have been called according to his purpose. For those God foreknew he also predestined to be conformed to the likeness of his Son, that he might be the firstborn among many brothers. And those he predestined, he also called; those he called, he also justified; those he justified, he also glorified.

It is only when we come to a true knowledge of ourselves, given us through the eyes of God, that we find a true peace and assurance of who we really are. Then we glimpse a true vision of what we can become through the transforming processes of Christ.

As Christians our hearts belong to the Lord Jesus, but we must allow the Lord to transform us daily by the renewing of our minds. As we do this, Scripture promises, the Lord will release benefits into our lives. The Lord just wants us to meet Him halfway, to be honest, to recognize our need for transformation: to turn our eyes and ears towards the wisdom that comes from the throne of grace. Yes, this is an ongoing process, it takes time to grow into the wisdom of God: and as we do we will discern, test and know the perfect plan of God for our lives, our families and our churches. Proverbs 2:2–6 encourages us:

> . . . turning your ear to wisdom
>   and applying your heart to understanding,
> and if you call out for insight
>   and cry aloud for understanding,
> and if you look for it as for silver

and search for it as for hidden treasure,
then you will understand the fear of the LORD
and find the knowledge of God.
For the LORD gives wisdom
and from his mouth come knowledge and
understanding.

(emphasis added)

Chapter 2

The
BENEFITS of
RENEWED MINDS

"For I know the plans I have for you," declares the LORD,
"plans to prosper you and not to harm you,
plans to give you hope and a future."
(Jeremiah 29:11)

When we incline our hearts and minds towards the Lord, He gives us blessings. His great delight is to encourage us as we please Him in our lives. As He ministers this to us we begin to learn what pleases Him, and the attitudes that honor Him. It is similar to how we are with our own children. I am a father with four children. When I see them growing and learning in the right ways, I encourage them. When I see them learning about family life and putting others before themselves, I positively reinforce this selfless behavior. A word of encouragement and love is worth a thousand words of harsh chastisement. There are still times when chastisement is needed, but right behavior needs encouragement.

When we renew our minds in the thoughts of God, we find many blessings. The Lord wants to minister to those who submit their wills to Him. There are pathways of encouragement that give us a greater quality of life than if we do things as we have always done them, our way. The Lord encourages those who seek after His own heart and live their lives in the wisdom He has for them. As a result we find benefits for us, if we cultivate minds renewed in the wisdom of God.

One benefit of minds that are being renewed is to test and approve God's plan for our lives. This is important to us, because one of the big questions that people ask is how to know God's purpose. The Lord's plan for our lives is better for us than any we can make for ourselves. His plan matches perfectly who we are as people, our strengths and weaknesses, and what is achievable for us as His people. Therefore to know and move in the plan of God is essential if we are to reach our full potential as Christians. But this discernment is only given to those who renew their minds in His wisdom. The wonderful truth is that He has a specific plan for each one of us, a plan that will bring good things into our lives. Jeremiah 29:11 gives us the promise of this plan, a plan to prosper us and not to harm us, a plan to give us hope and a future.

We are not here on earth by accident. Every one of us is part of God's plan because Scripture declares that the Lord governed our birth, and He has established the length of our days. Psalm 139 tells us how the Lord is involved not only in our creation, but also in our future:

> For you created my inmost being;
>   you knit me together in my mother's womb . . .
> All the days ordained for me
>   were written in your book
>   before one of them came to be.
>
> (Psalm 139:13, 16)

The Lord has a personal knowledge of us because He is the one who created us, governed our birth, and ordained our lifespan. He has a plan mapped out to bring us blessing, peace and fulfillment as we reach our full potential in Him. As Ephesians 2:10 says:

For we are God's workmanship, created in Christ Jesus to do good works, which God prepared in advance for us to do.

Here is the wonderful truth for your life and mine: the Lord has saved us for a purpose. He has established our lives in Him with a plan, a destiny for us to fulfill. Our ongoing life in Jesus means discerning that plan for our individual life, our family life, our work life and our church life. Without this sense of purpose we find that even as Christians we lack direction. This perfect plan of God, to prosper us and give us a hope and a future, is to be lived out in our everyday circumstances.

When we come to Jesus we no longer belong to ourselves, but to Him. The Lord places a calling upon us to fulfill purposes that He has entrusted into our hands. Every Christian has this calling upon his or her life, to go where Jesus tells him or her to go, to do what Jesus calls him or her to do. It is about doing the right job that He guides you to, then doing it in His way. It is about staying single, or marrying the right person as God has ordained. If the latter, it is about building a marriage and family life on the foundation of God and His purposes for you. This is not some token gesture by God, but something He trusts us with and expects us to do. The Lord shapes us as His people, that we might do the good works He has offered us. As we fulfill God's calling on our lives we bring glory to God, and He brings our lives to their full potential. As Colossians 3:23–24 says:

> Whatever you do, work at it with all your heart, as working for the Lord, not for men, since you know that you will receive an inheritance from the Lord as a reward. It is the Lord Christ you are serving.

We must let go of what the world tells us, let go of our own plans and desires, and give the future to the Lord. If we are prepared to cultivate a mind taught by God, then His perfect plan for our lives will be played out in our future. Knowing the will of God for our lives, and seeing His good plans manifested in our lives, we can grow in faith and potential as children of God. Our lives are opened up to the Lord's supernatural provision, so that we can succeed in His purposes. As we work out the plan of God in the small events of everyday life, the Lord opens up greater opportunities to serve and honor Him.

Another benefit of renewed minds is to live a life worthy and pleasing to Jesus. In any truly loving relationship there is a desire to please the other person by the way that you live. We want to do things to bless them, and behave in ways that honor them. In the same way the Lord knows our hearts' desire to live lives worthy and pleasing to Him. He knows that we long to know Him better, and to serve Him with greater joy. The result of this transforming process is for us to live daily lives pleasing to the Lord. Colossians 1:9–10 says:

> . . . we have not stopped praying for you and asking God to fill you with the knowledge of his will through all spiritual wisdom and understanding. And we pray this in order that you may live a life worthy of the Lord and may please him in every way: bearing fruit in every good work, growing in the knowledge of God.

This passage is clear about living a life pleasing to God, bearing good fruit, and growing in His power. We gain these things through a greater knowledge of God, by a release of wisdom that trains the heart and mind. Jesus has called us to holy living and given us many promises that are conditional on our right responses to Him each day. Our minds learn God's way, which releases a deep empowerment for daily righteous living. God's wisdom enables us to please Him in the way we live, so we grow in power, maturity and fruitfulness. Jesus Himself made it clear that He desires His people to be abundant in the kingdom fruit that they bear, because we thereby show ourselves to be His disciples.

The joy of our Christian lives is to be changed by the Holy Spirit to become more and more like Jesus. A disciple in the days of Jesus would live almost every moment of every day with his teacher. He would learn His teaching, and model His behavior. He would cultivate His attitudes, and strive in every way to please Him. Today, we Christians have the presence of the Holy Spirit within us, and He is the One who writes the laws of God upon our hearts. He is the One who, through teaching and conviction, leads us down the pathway of righteous living and enables us over time to be salt and light in this world. As we co-operate with the Holy Spirit and submit our preconceived morals and behavior to the Lord, He creates within us Christ-like minds and lifestyles that please Jesus and enable us to be ambassadors of His good news. There is no greater joy as children of God than knowing that our lives are pleasing to the One who has carried our guilt, paid our debt, and made us new creations though faith.

A further benefit of minds renewed in the wisdom of God is for our lives to be protected by Him. There are many hazards that would hurt and obstruct us as God's people. However, it is made clear in the Word of God that if we build our lives upon God's wisdom, then He will establish His victory in our lives. This does not mean that we will never go through difficult or trying times. It does not mean that we will never be persecuted for our faith, *but* that when we are we will be made overcomers of the evil in this world by the word of our testimony and the blood of the Lamb. Proverbs 2:7–8, in the context of seeking godly wisdom, promises us this:

> He holds victory in store for the upright,
>> he is a shield to those whose walk is blameless,
> for he guards the course of the just
>> and protects the way of his faithful ones.

Those who are just and faithful are those who know the will of the Lord and do it. They seek the Lord with all their hearts, and seek not only to know His way but to put it into practical daily obedience. Scripture declares that Jesus has come to defeat all the works of the evil one. He has come to make us people who overcome the evil of this world with good, and overcome hate with love. This scripture assures us that those who live in God's wisdom will be made secure in the things of the Kingdom, as we look to follow and serve our Savior.

This victory is about seeing God's purposes made manifest in our lives, and deepening our ongoing relationship with Jesus as we live each day for Him. Whatever we endure, we live in the knowledge that God will work out all things for the good of those who love Him. Even if our lives are taken from us, we have resurrection, we have life everlasting, and we have eternity with our Father in heaven. Yes, there will be times of trial and challenge, but we will overcome these trials by the keeping power of God and the authority of the Lamb. In Jesus our life and future as Christians is secure, and no weapon that is levelled against us by the devil or the world will ultimately prosper against us. This protection, this keeping power, is promised to those who seek and establish God's wisdom for their lives.

There are many other benefits of having our lives transformed by the renewing of our minds, and a wonderful summary is found in Proverbs 3. We need it to motivate our desire for growth, as we aspire to the wisdom of God. We find in this scripture great benefits, the fruit of allowing God to teach and shape us as His children. Remember, this passage came from Solomon, who was given by the Lord a gift of wisdom and knowledge:

> ... for they will prolong your life many years
> and bring you prosperity ...
> Then you will win favor and a good name
> in the sight of God and man.
> Trust in the LORD with all your heart
> *and lean not on your own understanding;*
> in all your ways acknowledge him,
> and he will make your paths straight.
>
> (Proverbs 3:2, 5–6, emphasis added)

The Hebrew word for "direct" here is *yashar*, which means that God will make your life straight, right, upright, pleasing, good. The promise here is of a life, a heart, a family that is good, upright and pleasing, not only to ourselves but also to the Lord. This is what godly wisdom offers to those who seek it. Yet the Proverb goes even further. Verse 8 says that if we shun evil, fear the Lord and are not puffed up with our own knowledge, then there will be "health to your body and nourishment to your bones." And finally in verse 10 we see that not only will our own needs be met, but there will be an overflow of blessings to others.

These promises are given to show us the better ways, the better wisdom of God for our lives. As we read them through and allow an understanding given us by the Holy Spirit of the character of God, our hearts may be led to joyful and expectant obedience. We see that even in God's Kingdom there are laws of cause and effect. If we build our lives on these things then the Lord will bless and prosper our lives. There may be times of hardship or difficulty, but the Lord promises to use all things for our long-term good. We see verse 13 in essence saying to us that true joy, and peace that cannot be shaken, are found in following the way of God and knowing His wisdom for our lives. The reason for all these things is that true wisdom, wisdom that lasts and does not change, has its origins in the Lord God Almighty. As Job says: "To God belong wisdom and power; counsel and understanding are his" (Job 12:13).

Our Lord has established the universe by His wisdom and knowledge. This same wisdom and knowledge He has made available to His people, if we are prepared to cultivate minds renewed in Him.

I have had the joy of knowing people who by the world's standards are not clever or intelligent, and yet over the years I have seen them come to an impressive level of wisdom and discernment in their lives as they have absorbed the Word of God and allowed His Holy Spirit to teach them. I have seen people go on to Bible college, and even confound their lecturers by the deep understanding they have had in the plans and purposes of God. The reason for this is that they have been fully open to allow the Holy Spirit to renew their minds in Christ Jesus.

We need to recognize how human knowledge has shaped our understanding, how we impose that understanding onto the things and purposes of the Kingdom, and how this often results in double-mindedness. We must allow the Spirit of God to open up our hearts and minds to the everlasting knowledge of the Lord Almighty. Are you willing right now, today, to say to yourself and to the Lord: "Yes Lord, I commit myself to cultivate a mind that is renewed in Your knowledge and in Your ways"? Are you prepared to say today: "Lord, give me Your wisdom and plans that I might live a life that is worthy of You"? As Proverbs 3 tells us:

> Surely He scorns the scornful,
> But gives grace to the humble.
> The wise shall inherit glory . . .

> (Proverbs 3:34–35 NKJV)

Chapter 3

GROWING *in* the MIND *of* CHRIST

*"For who has known the mind of the Lord
that he may instruct him?"*

But we have the mind of Christ.

(1 Corinthians 2:16)

We need to understand as God's children that the Lord will provide everything we need to be effective as His people. As people who belong to Jesus, we are called to go out into the world and bear witness to Him. This means that we need to behave in such a way that the people of the world see real Kingdom living. To live as Kingdom people takes a wisdom that comes only from the King of kings and the Lord of lords.

One joy of being a Christian is that the Lord promises each of us a resource of knowledge that comes from the very heart of Jesus Himself. He wants us, as children of our heavenly Father, to know what is on His mind and His heart, and to be obedient to what He calls us to do. Here is the wonderful truth of being a Christian: the Lord's wisdom is available to each of us, so that we might know all He wants us to know.

Scripture makes it clear that there is a hidden-ness in the things of the Kingdom, in the mind of Christ. *But* that hidden-ness is directed at the lost and the proud. Jesus declares that the demonic things of this world blind and deafen people to the truth of the Kingdom. In Matthew 13:11–17 He helps us to understand the wisdom and knowledge of the Kingdom, and how its revelation is given into our lives:

> He replied, "The knowledge of the secrets of the kingdom of heaven has been given to you, but not to them."
>
> (Matthew 13:11)

> "Though seeing, they do not see;
>   though hearing, they do not hear or understand."
>
> (Matthew 13:13)

He goes on to say that we have come into this wonderful truth that many who have gone before us have desired to see, yet have not. Paul also shows us the real spiritual blindness that afflicts the lost. In 2 Corinthians 4:4 he writes:

> The god of this age has blinded the minds of unbelievers, so that they cannot see the light of the gospel of the glory of Christ, who is the image of God.

This is an important verse to us because it declares that when we go out and share the good news of Jesus, we need to cover everything in prayer. The blindness in many people's lives is a spiritual condition, and therefore we need to pray in the Spirit for these people, so that the conviction of the Spirit will heal their blindness and deafness, and through that same conviction their sin will be challenged. Amazingly, all the Lord intends for His people is written down in His Word, the Bible. We can take a Bible and read it, and it is plain for all to see what the Lord ordains. Yet without spiritual eyes and spiritual ears we can see and never perceive, hear and never understand. The Father wants to give wisdom to people, but that wisdom is only made manifest to those who truly belong to Him, and who are led by His Holy Spirit.

As a minister a lot of my work focuses on families, and I often get to know several generations of the same family. It is interesting to observe how often different generations will say the same things in the same ways. Such sayings have been passed down the generations. We all promise ourselves that we won't become like our mums and dads and say the things that were said to us, yet as the years pass we catch ourselves saying to our children just what our parents said to us! My grandma used to say "A watched pot never boils," "You'll catch your death of cold by walking around like that," and "If the wind changes your face will stick like that." We all know that there is little truth in the old wives' tales that have been passed down to us, but we see that family knowledge and wisdom are still passed down from one generation to the next. Sometimes this is done for fun, and sometimes to be a practical help to those who succeed us.

As part of the family of God, we see that the Father wants to pass on to us, His children by adoption, His knowledge – not only about the unchanging reality of His Word, but also about the practical situations of our lives, and His plans for us. In the new covenant that the Lord has established through Christ's blood, we have a new relationship with the Father by being born again spiritually. God wants to pour out His wisdom into our lives so that we may live powerfully for Him. The words of Isaiah 55:8 – " 'For my thoughts are not your thoughts, neither are your ways my ways,' declares the LORD" – are true for the old covenant, but not for the new covenant established in Jesus. It is true for knowledge that comes from outside oneself, but not for those who are taught in the knowledge of the Word by the indwelling presence of the Holy Spirit.

Many Christians quote this verse to explain why we do not understand certain experiences in our lives. Preachers often use the verse to state that we cannot know the thoughts and ways of God. They overlook the truth that this verse is centered in the old covenant, from a time before the Holy Spirit was poured out by the Messiah on to all who believe in Him. The old covenant is the state of those who do not have their minds transformed by the renewing power of the Holy Spirit. If this is your condition as a Christian, then you are living in ignorance of all that you have been offered through Jesus Christ. One of the works of the Messiah, the anointed one of God, is giving us the Holy Spirit and thereby writing the laws of God on our hearts and minds:

> "This is the covenant that I will make with
>   the house of Israel
>   after that time," declares the LORD.
> "I will put my law in their minds
>   and write it on their hearts.
> I will be their God,
>   and they will be my people."

(Jeremiah 31:33)

Through the gift of the Holy Spirit we can discover great depths of wisdom from the mind of Christ that was not commonly available to the people of the old covenant. Then, the Holy Spirit had not yet been poured out on all flesh. Yes, they had the law and the Ten Commandments, but this was an external law that could be kept without filtering down to the heart and bringing true revelation. The law was not an outward sign of an inner purity towards God and one another in community: the law became legalism in the hearts of God's people. This outward obedience affected the behavior of the individual, but did not result in a real change of heart towards God.

In the book of Amos we see that many of the actions that the Lord calls His people to do, He actually rejects, because their hearts are hard and there is no mercy, justice or wisdom in what they do. Yes, they kept the feasts and festivals of the Lord, but their hearts remained unconverted to the truth. So wisdom did not govern their lives, justice did not govern their actions, and mercy did not govern their help to those in need. Amos 5:21–24 describes God's anger:

"I hate, I despise your religious feasts;
   I cannot stand your assemblies.
Even though you bring me burnt offerings and
      grain offerings,
   I will not accept them.
Though you bring choice fellowship offerings,
   I will have no regard for them.
Away with the noise of your songs!
   I will not listen to the music of your harps.
But let justice roll on like a river,
   righteousness like a never-failing stream!"

We see here that the law was meant to bring wisdom and revelation to the hearts of God's people, to show them how to live righteous lives before the Lord, and how to care for one another. Yet this external law became a witness against their unconverted hearts, and against the pride of their ways. Amos reminds us that the one true God is perfect, and He does not sin. He is holy, He hates evil and will not look upon sin. Now here is the problem: we are sinners who do wrong, acting in selfish and evil ways. The heart of our problem today is that we are born into a world, a society, a life that is saturated by the sin of Adam. Romans 5:12 teaches us that "sin entered the world through one man, and death through sin, and in this way death came to all men, because all sinned." The sin in our lives is an abomination in the eyes of a pure God, and results in death. This is not just futility of heart: our minds are also "unprofitable" in the things of the Kingdom. As Romans 3:10–11 tells us:

"There is no-one righteous, not even one;
   there is no-one who understands,
   no-one who seeks God.

All have turned away,
    they have together become worthless;
there is no-one who does good,
    not even one."

Verses 22–23 add:

> . . . There is no difference, for all have sinned and fall short of
> the glory of God.

Here is our problem before we accept Jesus as Lord and Savior.
God is righteous but we are unrighteous, a broken people
under judgment, with no way back to the Father. This was
the state humanity was in before Jesus – unable to earn
salvation, or to do enough religious duty to cancel out the debt
we owe to God. But the wonderful truth is that in Jesus, God's
righteousness has been revealed. It is a righteousness that
comes to us as a powerful initiative of God's love and grace. A
righteousness apart from the law has been revealed, and is
manifested in our lives through living faith in Jesus Christ. This
means a rightness that is not dependent on our rituals or good
works or goodness, but a rightness *with God* that is given to us
as we walk our faith in the resurrection of Jesus. This righteousness is given when we repent of our sin, and accept Jesus
Christ as Lord and Savior.

Our problem as human beings is that we need more than
something to believe in, we need more than a sense of
acceptance and love. The Word makes it clear that we need a
new relationship with the God who made us. To enable this we
need someone who will rescue us from sin, from Satan, from
death, from the judgment and punishment of God. In short, we
need a new nature. Jesus is the atoning sacrifice who through the
shedding of His blood frees us from past sin. As Scripture says:
"whom God set forth as a propitiation by His blood, [How?]
through faith, to demonstrate [What?] His righteousness"
(Romans 3:25 NKJV).

It was the blood of Jesus that paid the debt of sin, released us from the prison of death, and enabled us to be spiritually born again. Jesus became a sacrificial offering to take our sin, guilt and punishment upon Himself. When He died on the cross, all the punishment and wrath of God was directed at the sin in Him. In 1 Peter 2:24 we read:

> He himself bore our sins in his body on the tree, so that we might die to sins and live for righteousness; by his wounds you have been healed.

He became the scapegoat, so our sin and guilt have been paid for. Jesus took our place in the courtroom of God, was condemned for our sin, and took upon Himself our punishment. Therefore we stand before Him as righteous because our sin has been removed, our guilt paid for, and our punishment borne by Jesus – all because of the blood of the new covenant that was poured out for us.

It is the power of the blood of Jesus that saves, cleanses, purifies and makes us right with God. It is the blood of Jesus, applied by repentance and faith, that unites us in relationship with God and entitles us to God's salvation. The blood of Jesus is forever the only means by which we can come into a right relationship with God. Hebrews 9 helps us understand the eternal value and sufficiency of the blood of Jesus. Verses 14 and 15 tell us:

> How much more, then, will the blood of Christ, who through the eternal Spirit offered himself unblemished to God, cleanse our consciences from acts that lead to death, so that we may serve the living God!
>
> For this reason Christ is the mediator of a new covenant, that those who are called may receive the promised eternal inheritance – now that he has died as a ransom to set them free from the sins committed under the first covenant.

Scripture makes it clear that an internal work of revelation needs to be manifested in the lives of those whom the Lord had chosen for His salvation. This new revelation would not just be an external work of education, but an internal transformation of hearts and minds through the Holy Spirit. It would take place within the children of God as the promised ministry of the Messiah was made real in the outpouring of the Holy Spirit. When we received the baptism of the Holy Spirit we became the temple of the Holy Spirit, our teacher and guide, who took from Jesus and made it known to us. John 16:12–15 quotes Jesus:

> "I have much more to say to you, more than you can now bear. But when he, the Spirit of truth, comes, he will guide you into all truth. He will not speak on his own; he will speak only what he hears, and he will tell you what is yet to come. He will bring glory to me by taking from what is mine and making it known to you. All that belongs to the Father is mine. That is why I said the Spirit will take from what is mine and make it known to you."

This promise is an amazing statement of intent from the mouth of Jesus Himself. All wisdom and knowledge, in the whole universe, belongs to the Father, the Lord God Almighty, and also to the Son, for the Son and the Father are one. Now here is the Son Jesus declaring that by the pouring out of the Holy Spirit, who is one with the Father and the Son, you and I will be taught all wisdom and knowledge in the Lord. All that the Father has belongs to Jesus, and Jesus says that for those who have the Holy Spirit as teacher, they will be open to know all things as the Lord ordains. Here is an astonishing promise of wisdom. For those who will walk with the Holy Spirit, being transformed by the renewing of their minds, there is a promise of continuous understanding from the Lord. When we think what this means, when we begin to take in the depth of what Jesus is offering us, there is no end to the possibilities that the wisdom of God can open up for our lives.

It does not matter how clever we are in the world's terms. If we open our hearts and minds to the Word of God and allow the Holy Spirit to teach us, Scripture declares that the Lord's discernment will be made available to inform and govern our lives. In spiritual terms the Lord levels the playing field, making His wisdom available to all who cultivate a life founded on His Spirit and Word. Spiritual wisdom is not just available to the minister or the scholar, but to all in the body of Christ who are willing to be transformed by the renewing of their minds. It means that the Lord can speak His wisdom to all of us, through all who belong to Christ, no matter what worldly qualifications a person has. I have been in situations where ministers have been corrected, encouraged and taught by even the youngest in faith, as the Holy Spirit has given them utterance.

I know that for some, this will seem incredible. Some will dismiss it as a text taken out of context. Let those who are spiritual discern what the Word of God promises the children of God. In the context of salvation, 1 Corinthians 2 promises us the same unlimited wisdom that Jesus has. Here Paul talks about a hidden knowledge of God that is known to the spiritually mature. It is not hidden in the sense of not being spoken of, but in the sense that it needs to be spiritually discerned.

I have had the privilege of preaching in many churches in my time as a Christian. In one particular Methodist chapel I had a long conversation with the organist, who was paid to play the hymns chosen that Sunday. He had been taught to play by his father, and was used in the area by several churches which needed an organist. The interesting thing is that this man confessed himself to be an atheist. He had sat through hundreds of sermons over many years, had heard sermons by many preachers, and yet remained unconvinced by any of it. He was a man forever hearing but never perceiving.

Paul makes it clear in 1 Corinthians 2:10–16 that there is a wisdom and understanding given by the Holy Spirit to those who belong to Jesus. Verses 10–12 give us a wonderful truth about the all-knowing wisdom of the Spirit: that wisdom is given to us because we have received not the spirit of the world, but the Spirit who is from God. Listen to these words with an open heart, and ask what this truth means in the context of a renewed mind in Christ:

> The Spirit searches all things, even the deep things of God. For who among men knows the thoughts of a man except the man's spirit within him? *In the same way* no-one knows the thoughts of God except the Spirit of God.
>
> (1 Corinthians 2:10–11, emphasis added)

Can we agree that the Holy Spirit who is *one* with the Father and the Son knows all that the Father knows and understands? If we can, and this is the same Holy Spirit whom we receive by faith in the Lord Jesus, then great wisdom is made available to us as children of God. Indeed verses 12–13 make it clear that this is the same Holy Spirit who knows the deep things of the Father:

> We have not received the spirit of the world but the Spirit who is from God, that we may understand what God has freely given us. This is what we speak, not in words taught us by human wisdom but in words taught by the Spirit, expressing spiritual truths in spiritual words.

Paul gives us a clear testimony that the promises of Jesus have come true for him, in that the Holy Spirit has become his teacher. Paul makes it clear that the wisdom of what he writes comes through the revelation of the Holy Spirit, and that these revelations need to be discerned through the Holy Spirit.

We must stay humble in the possibilities that the Lord gives us, recognizing that there is no greater revelation to us than Scripture itself. Scripture is the plumb-line, the test, the full revelation of the plans and purposes of God, and therefore any revelation we think we have from the Lord needs to be tested against the perfect standard of the Word. If anything is added to or taken away from the revelation of Scripture by what we feel has been revealed to us, then the latter is *not* of God and therefore false. Even in the joy of the Lord's promises there must be a warning against pride, a call to be humble before the Lord and His truth. What has been revealed needs a humble and biblically sensitive response, in order to discern its weight and power.

Even with the guidance and revelation of the Holy Spirit, what we understand about the Lord is very small. His mind is beyond measure, and we could take a thousand lifetimes of learning to scratch the surface. He is the One who spoke the universe into existence, who sustains all things by His active will and mighty power, who controls the times and the seasons, who keeps the universe in existence. All these things the Lord has done through His wisdom. Every creature was made by Him, is known and sustained by Him. No one was His teacher, no one showed Him how to create. All true wisdom is found only in its source, the Lord God Almighty.

Our fragile minds do not have the capacity to understand the Lord and His ways. But led by the Spirit who expands our minds, we can understand all that the Lord wants us to concerning His purposes. We can know the full revelation found within His Word. He wants us to be free, open to the direction that comes through the Holy Spirit, to obey His perfect will for our lives. He wants all of us who love Him to move in the wisdom of the mind of Christ. The Holy Spirit nurtures this, for it is God's will that we should have the mind of Christ. Verse 16 says that no one before Jesus has known His mind. No one has truly known the thoughts of God before the outpouring of the Holy Spirit. Even Solomon, in all the wisdom given to him by the Lord, had things hidden from him.

But we have the mind of Christ.

(1 Corinthians 2:16)

Who has known the mind of God? No one, until the mind of Christ was revealed in the lives of the children of God.

This teaching is not some fringe doctrine of the given-ness of God's wisdom. It is core Christian belief, available to every follower of Jesus who has repented of his or her sin, accepted Jesus Christ as Lord and Savior, and been baptized in His Holy Spirit. God wants to create the mind of Christ in our lives so that we might know all that He has given us, rejoice in the God of our salvation, and live out His plans in our everyday lives. He has given us His Spirit to make wisdom real in the lives of all who trust in Him. As we grow in spiritually discerned knowledge, we find an increasing manifestation of the attitude and morality of Jesus in our lives. As we read the Word of God we begin to understand its teaching from a spiritual perspective, and to know the purposes of God. These are then enacted in our lives as we allow the Holy Spirit to inform our thinking.

God wants us to cultivate His wisdom in our lives, and He gives us permission to ask for it. James 1:5–8 tell us:

> If any of you lacks wisdom, he should ask God, who gives generously to all without finding fault, *and it will be given to him.* But when he asks, he must believe and not doubt, because he who doubts is like a wave of the sea, blown and tossed by the wind. That man should not think he will receive anything from the Lord; he is a double-minded man, unstable in all he does.
>
> (emphasis added)

The promise here from the Lord is that *it will be given* to us when we ask for wisdom. Why? Because wisdom is the Lord's intention for all His children. To know God's ways, to understand God's decrees, to live our lives in line with His will and purposes, are all part of the wonderful relationship we have been created for in Christ. Therefore there is no need to go through life guessing the way we should walk or the choices we should make. There is no need to be fearful of making the wrong decisions, or being double-minded when we make decisions. The Lord encourages us to ask for what we need, so that we can be in the center of His will. He opens up for us the promise of His wisdom to inform our choices, if we are prepared to ask Him for that. Wisdom will be given us because it is the Father's intention that the mind of Christ should be revealed in our lives. If we are prepared to journey down pathways of lives that are pleasing to the Lord, then He is prepared to open up His mind to ours. As Ecclesiastes 2:26 says: "To the man who pleases him, God gives wisdom, knowledge and happiness . . . "

Chapter 4

CHOOSING WHAT
INFLUENCES US

Finally, brothers, whatever is true, whatever is noble,
whatever is right, whatever is pure, whatever is lovely,
whatever is admirable – if anything is excellent
or praiseworthy – think about such things.
(Philippians 4:8)

When we consider how to grow in the wisdom of God, it is essential to realize that our choices influence how deeply and quickly we grow in the mind of Christ. Our choices affect our minds, our morals and ultimately our decisions. We need to understand that what we choose to soak up in our lives has a direct effect on the condition of our hearts and the depth of our faith. In fact, in the context of renewed minds we see that how we entertain ourselves, and the people we choose to mix with, can block or release God's wisdom in our lives. In Philippians 4:8 Paul warns us that the way we choose to act is formed and cultivated in our minds first. Whatever we fill our minds with will affect our morality, our desires and our decisions. Who we spend time with will have an effect on our behavior and life choices. What we bring into our lives through the music we listen to, and the films and TV programs we watch, will subtly affect our spirituality. This is why Paul gives us godly criteria to evaluate influences out there in the world, and therefore choose what we are prepared to bring into our lives as Christians.

To renew our minds, there are practical initiatives we can take to develop godly wisdom more quickly. But be clear that there is a cost in saying no to the immoral things of this world, and many of the ways that we entertain ourselves have values that are worldly and sinful. To say no to the latest blockbuster movie, or turn down other opportunities to fulfill sinful desires, takes self-discipline and a focus on loving the Lord Jesus and honoring Him first in our lives. It may mean that we're seen as strange or fanatical, even by some in the church, because we do not indulge in the same things as the people of the world. Even Christian newspapers and magazines encourage their readers to see a particular sinful film or engage in a compromised viewpoint. They tell us to do this so that we can "fit in". However, when we fill our lives with the rubbish of the world we find that the beautiful wisdom of the Lord becomes smothered and stunted in our lives.

If we live a daily life that is right with God, then He will bring into our lives the blessings that we find within His Word. Jesus has made us right through faith in His resurrection. He has taken our place, paid our debt, and endured our punishment so that now we stand before the Lord Almighty in a right relationship with Him. Now the daily challenge laid before us is to live in the fullness of that right relationship we have been saved to enjoy.

It is by the choices we make each day that this righteousness grows, blessing our lives in Jesus. Our choices help in either renewing our minds in Christ, or hindering that growth. Scripture shows that lifestyle rightness with God means turning our backs on sins like greed, unforgiveness, anger, selfishness, pride and lust; and choosing to obey the Word of the Lord in the choices we make and the lives we live. By the renewing of our minds we learn to walk in this rightness every day, to live holy lives. We need to count ourselves dead to the wrong actions and attitudes of our weaker moments and focus on being alive, responsive to God in Christ Jesus. It is fundamentally important that we do not let sin take root in our desires, or we shall obey evil desires that grieve our relationship with the Lord.

We can quicken the pace of growth in godly wisdom by guarding our hearts and minds against the rubbish that this world throws at us. On an average night of television we can soak up appalling images of sexual lust, violence, murder, rape, adultery, sex before marriage and greed. These things are common fare in TV programs or films, and even as Christians we accept them as the norm. From birth onwards, we and our children are bombarded with ungodly images promoting selfish greed, loose morals and disposable relationships. Even in children's programs there are elements of witchcraft and the supernatural. We see children engaging in relationships before they are ready, we see offensive and selfish behavior. I would encourage every parent to monitor what their children watch, for mainstream children's programs start our children on a diet of violence and the supernatural while they are very young. It amazes me how many Christians have jumped onto the *Harry Potter* bandwagon. Even Christian leaders declare with regular foolishness that there is nothing wrong with these books and films, and that they provide good lessons on morality, bravery and friendship. Unfortunately such Christian leaders are so impressed with the success of these books that they espouse a strategy of Satan to indoctrinate the next generation with a pagan worldview.

Many passages in Scripture speak of avoiding the occult, spiritism and witchcraft. Deuteronomy 18:9–12 is one of them:

> When you enter the land the LORD your God is giving you, *do not learn to imitate* the detestable ways of the nations there. Let no-one be found among you who sacrifices his son or daughter in the fire, who practices divination or sorcery, interprets omens, engages in witchcraft, or casts spells, or who

is a medium or spiritist or who consults the dead. Anyone who does these things is detestable to the LORD . . .

(emphasis added)

Although Scripture warns us about the danger of witchcraft and paganism, and Scripture calls us to guard our children and bring them up in the way of the Lord, many Christian parents have brought this occult worldview into their children's lives, and actively endorsed its influence over their young minds. The Pagan Federation have admitted that since the *Harry Potter* films were released they have over a hundred contacts a month from children, asking how they might train as witches and learn to cast spells. How many of these children are from nominally Christian families? All this may all seem a bit of harmless fun, but Scripture declares that what we take into our minds and hearts can affect our understanding for better or worse. Paul teaches that if we allow our minds and hearts to be filled with such rubbish, it will have both a subtle and a direct effect on our moral life, on the choices we make and the worldview we hold.

One problem for many Christians is that we want to be seen as just like everyone else. But the patterns of this world, the ways people entertain themselves, the things they aspire to in life, are influenced by (at best) the selfish desires of the human heart or (at worst) a demonic strategy to keep people too busy, too entertained, too focused on themselves to see the truth. We as God's people must understand that our identity, our inheritance, our citizenship do not come from this earth, but have been given to us and established for us in heaven. We are called to live lives devoted to Jesus Himself, seeking the wisdom that He brings into our lives by the Holy Spirit. We cannot serve two masters. We cannot serve God and man, and we cannot live lives copying the patterns of this world and expect them to be pleasing to God. What we take in through our eyes and ears shapes our desires, fears, hopes and behavior.

In both the Old and the New Testament it is clear that what

you fix your eyes on becomes the desire of your heart. Psalm 119:37 expresses the cry of the heart:

> Turn my eyes away from worthless things;
>   preserve my life according to your word.

If we want to see our minds renewed in the things of God then we need to do two things: to guard our thought lives, by choosing what we take into our minds.

A good piece of advice I was given as a young Christian was this: imagine that Jesus is walking by your side. When you are not sure whether to watch something, do something, say something, then ask yourself, "Would I be happy doing this, watching this, saying this, if Jesus was by my side?" In fact Jesus is by our side in a spiritual sense, because we are the temple of the Holy Spirit and He lives within us. As 1 Corinthians 3:16 says:

> Don't you know that you yourselves are God's temple and that God's Spirit lives in you? If anyone destroys God's temple, God will destroy him; for God's temple is sacred, and you are that temple.

Christian bookshops used to sell wristbands with the initials WWJD, standing for "What Would Jesus Do?" The challenge was: "Would you watch that horror film if Jesus was by your side? Would you be happy to read those sexual jokes if Jesus was by your side? Would you go to that website, or talk like that in that chat room, if Jesus was by your side? Would you gossip about that person with your friends, if Jesus was by your side? Would you listen to the lyrics of that song and think they were cool, if Jesus was by your side?"

If we are serious about gaining the wisdom of God, we need to guard our thought lives. We must have the courage to say no to films, programs, people and influences that will draw our thinking into the morality of this fallen world. As Jesus says, we are *in* this world but we are not *of* this world. We are called to witness to the lost, but we are not meant to engage in the same sinful activities that they themselves do. Whatever we are tempted to take into our lives, God gives us His standard for knowing what is good. Is it true, noble, right, admirable, excellent, praiseworthy? For these things lead us into pathways that help us discern the thoughts of the Lord. But the things of this world bind our thoughts and behavior to compromise, self-indulgence and sin.

As we guard our minds against unwholesome things, we also need to fix our minds on what is good. Our minds, as Christians, are not meant to be a vacuum, empty and unoccupied. In fact emptiness can be as dangerous as thinking about something sinful. Much of Eastern mysticism is focused on the idea of stilling ourselves and emptying our minds of all that might hinder us. This is dangerous because whatever encourages us to empty our minds and become passive in our wills has the potential to open our lives to the active influence of evil spirits. This is why yoga, hypnosis and many forms of Eastern meditation are warned against by Christians who deal with healing and deliverance. When we become passive in our minds we are open to any influence around us, including the demonic. Our passivity becomes a doorway through which our minds, spirits and lives can be influenced by deceiving spirits.

Scripture makes it clear that we should never empty our minds, so it is dangerous to use breathing and muscle techniques to relax our bodies to the point of submission. Sadly, many books about prayer and ancient Christian mysticism actively encourage Christians to engage in this worldly practice, and many are led astray by deceiving spirits. The Bible advises us about Christian meditation: fixing our minds on those things that renew our thinking, filling our minds with thoughts of God, and reflecting on His works and His ways towards us. We stimulate blessed thoughts as we read His Word, reflect upon His actions towards us, and remind ourselves of the wonder and majesty of His creation. In fixing our minds on the Lord we are looking to encounter the one true God in the seat of our understanding by focusing on the truth of His Word. This has a direct impact on our lives, if our minds are centered in God's wisdom.

There is a clear link between focus and outcome. Earthly things produce earthly wisdom, and man's wisdom is foolishness before an all-knowing and all-powerful God. Fixing our minds on heavenly things results in heavenly wisdom and leads to life-giving pathways for our lives. Scripture declares that God's wisdom is more valuable than silver or gold. To create these pathways of wisdom we must be prepared to assess the patterns of this world, and day by day cultivate a life that is good, right and true.

In Psalm 141 David shows us the truest place to keep our focus:

> But my eyes are fixed on you, O Sovereign LORD;
> in you I take refuge . . .
>
> (Psalm 141:8)

As we fill our lives up with worthy influences we establish spirits that are open, discerning and responsive to God's wisdom and truth. As we fix our eyes on the things of God and eschew the sin of this world, we begin to make straight paths for our lives. Proverbs 4:23–27 instructs us:

> Above all else, guard your heart,
>   for it is the wellspring of life.
> Put away perversity from your mouth;
>   keep corrupt talk far from your lips.
> Let your eyes look straight ahead,
>   fix your gaze directly before you.
> Make level paths for your feet
>   and take only ways that are firm.
> Do not swerve to the right or the left;
>   keep your foot from evil.

Whatever is true, good, right, pure, holy, praiseworthy, we are commanded to think only on such things. To some, this will be seen as fanatical and out of keeping with modern society and its trends. But in all these things it is God's way or no way. If we fill our lives with rubbish, then our hearts and minds will be tainted. It has been said many times: "garbage in – garbage out." Paul says it in his own way: "Do not conform any longer to the pattern of this world" (Romans 12:2). Can we hear what Paul is saying? Do not conform to the ways of this sinful world. If we mess around with the rubbish of this world, and lack the self-control to say no to things that oppose the Lord, then our lives as Christians will be tainted and His wisdom will not be made manifest.

Surveys have shown that while 90 percent of Christians watch the television for at least two hours every night, less then 25 percent of Christians read their Bibles more than once a week. So what is really influencing the hearts and minds of God's people in the church? Is it the world or the wisdom of God? Hebrews 12:1–2 gives us this advice about focusing our minds each day:

> . . . let us throw off everything that hinders and the sin that so easily entangles, and let us run with perseverance the race marked out for us. Let us fix our eyes on Jesus, the author and perfecter of our faith . . .

We need to take responsibility for ourselves, and co-operate with God's renewing process for us. We must say no to the rubbish of this world in its entertainment and its morality, and fix our eyes on Jesus, the author and finisher of our faith. If we are serious about laying hold on God's wisdom then we need to respond to St Paul's words:

> Finally, brothers, whatever is true, whatever is noble, whatever is right, whatever is pure, whatever is lovely, whatever is admirable – if anything is excellent or praiseworthy – think about such things.
>
> (Philippians 4:8)

Chapter 5

SETTING OUR MINDS *on* ETERNAL THINGS

Since, then, you have been raised with Christ,
set your hearts on things above, where Christ is seated
at the right hand of God. Set your minds on things above,
not on earthly things. For you died, and
your life is now hidden with Christ in God.
(Colossians 3:1–3)

As children of God, one of the important challenges in our lives is keeping our focus on what is to come. As Christians in this world, much of our life is focused on the here and now. We are encouraged to desire the immediacy of the moment. Why work for something long-term when you can have it right now? Many people, even Christians, have got themselves into massive debt because they have taken out loans to get what they want when they want it. We live in a "buy now pay later" society, and this is reflected in many of our attitudes to life. From fast food to instant pain relief, from easy loans to next day delivery, we are encouraged to focus on the moment and not to think about the long-term consequences. However, as children of God we need to understand that our promised inheritance in Christ is only given when we see Jesus face to face. We are encouraged by the Word to see that this world is not our home. We are traveling through this life, simultaneously living for Jesus and keeping our focus on what is to come.

I remember a TV interview with a famous sprinter who had just won Olympic gold. The sports reporter asked him why he seemed to be so serious and focused at the start of the race. The athlete replied that he looked down his lane to the finish line. He allowed the noise of the crowd and the athletes around him to fade into the background, focused on his own lane, and visualized the race he would run. He said: "When I look down my lane I am completely blinkered. I focus on the finishing line, replaying that moment when I will break that ribbon to the cries and cheers of the crowd." The sportsman was saying that even in the midst of great distractions before a big race, his absolute focus was on the goal of finishing first.

We as the Lord's people need to have the same determination and focus, to take our eyes off the distracting voices and philosophies of this world, and fix our hearts on the goal of our faith which is Jesus Christ. This man trained his mind against distractions so that he might win the applause and temporary rewards of this world. How much more should we train our hearts and minds in the things of the Kingdom? What we find in Jesus lasts forever. In 2 Corinthians 4 and 5 we find some wonderful insight into the reality of what we are now, and what we will ultimately become in Christ. It gives us great encouragement that the Lord Himself has promised to establish a home for us through Jesus: all who trust in the Lord will be changed in the twinkling of an eye from what is mortal to what is eternal. We need to listen to some of these wonderful verses, and allow the Holy Spirit to give us an eternal perspective to our everyday lives.

> Therefore we do not lose heart. Though outwardly we are wasting away, yet inwardly we are being renewed day by day. For our light and momentary troubles are achieving for us an eternal glory that far outweighs them all. So we fix our eyes

not on what is seen, but on what is unseen. For what is seen is temporary, but what is unseen is eternal.

(2 Corinthians 4:16–18)

Now we know that if the earthly tent we live in is destroyed, we have a building from God, an eternal house in heaven, not built by human hands.

(2 Corinthians 5:1)

Now it is God who has made us for this very purpose and has given us the Spirit as a deposit, guaranteeing what is to come.

(2 Corinthians 5:5)

The Lord gives us a pearl of great price: that should define not only our actions, but also the focus of our hearts and minds. As Christians we have a choice: we can be drawn into the insecurities of this life and allow them to create fears and anxieties in our lives. We can fix our minds on these things that are temporary, or on that which lasts forever. The word in this passage for "fix" actually means "look at, contemplate, keep your eye on, observe and watch." So what is being said here is that we should fix our eyes on, contemplate, and keep our eyes on that which is eternal.

Our lives are indeed very fragile, there is a "here today gone tomorrow" quality about all of us. Most of us have pictures of recent ancestors who are no longer with us. You only have to go back two hundred years to see that everyone who lived on the earth then is no longer with us. Many of us have trees in our gardens that were there before we were born and will be there long after we have gone. As 1 Peter 1:23–25 says:

For you have been born again, not of perishable seed, but of imperishable, through the living and enduring word of God. For,

"All men are like grass,
and all their glory is like the flowers of the field;
the grass withers and the flowers fall,
but the word of the Lord stands forever."

It makes no sense to focus our hearts and minds on what will not last. If we fix our hearts on these temporary things then we will be insecure, because deep down we know that they are here today and gone tomorrow.

As I grow older it seems to me that everyone wants to sell you something to help your future. For example, when you get a job you are offered different pension plans to help you plan your retirement. When you get married you are offered life insurance, to protect your wife if something happens to you. When you have children you are offered policies to pay for their education. When you get into your forties you are offered health insurance, and they play on the growing size of your waist-line to persuade you. When you get into your fifties they want to sell you "whole-life" plans to provide for your funeral expenses, or leave a nice little sum for your family and, by the way, you get a free pen and clock-radio when you sign up!

Much of what we do to secure our future is a happy illusion, giving us a false sense of security. Many people, even some Christians, think that the getting of these things will bring security and safety to their lives. Often we can make our focus the rewards of life, ambitions, dreams, as if somehow these things can give some eternal benefit. Much "prosperity" theology peddled to the Christian world encourages us to chase these things. False teachers in the church encourage God's people to put our hope in this world, our trust in our possessions, our security in our wealth.

However, the words of Jesus make it clear that anything we can earn or achieve on this earth will do us no good when it comes to eternity. Wealth, fame, status, achievement, even possessions, are fleeting glories that turn to dust in the face of death and eternity. Jesus says in Matthew 6:19: "Do not store up for yourselves treasures on earth, where moth and rust destroy, and where thieves break in and steal."

I remember watching a documentary on the ancient Egyptians, who believed that they could take the things of this world into the afterlife. So they would bury the dead with all their wealth, gold and jewelry. Even their slaves and animals were entombed. We all know what happened to this false hope. Thousands of years later some archaeologist discovers the burial site, takes all the wealth, gold and jewelry, gives it to a museum or sells it to a private collector, and even puts the body on public display for all to see. If only the ancient Egyptians had had the wisdom of my old grandma, who declared: "You can't take it with you when you're gone."

The more we put our trust in temporary things, the more we hold on to material things, the more we place our confidence in the things of the world – the more we buy into a false hope that cannot save us in eternity! Scripture often reminds us that hope in the things of this world is a false security, which will fade away with time and crumble in the face of adversity. Listen to what Scripture says concerning the "here today gone tomorrow" security of this world. Let the Word of God renew our minds, our thoughts and our focus as we look to build our lives on what Jesus has given us:

> Naked a man comes from his mother's womb,
>   and as he comes, so he departs.
> He takes nothing from his labor
>   that he can carry in his hand.
>
> (Ecclesiastes 5:15)

> "Man born of woman
>   is of few days and full of trouble.
> He springs up like a flower and withers away;
>   like a fleeting shadow, he does not endure."
>
> (Job 14:1–2)

> Do not be overawed when a man grows rich,
>   when the splendor of his house increases;
> for he will take nothing with him when he dies...
>
> (Psalm 49:16–17)

In James 1:10–11 we see a comparison between the one whose trust is in this world, and the one whose trust is in Jesus:

> But the one who is rich should take pride in his low position, because he will pass away like a wild flower. For the sun rises with scorching heat and withers the plant; its blossom falls and its beauty is destroyed. In the same way, the rich man will fade away even while he goes about his business.

Now listen to the wonderful truth of life found in Jesus:

> Blessed is the man who perseveres under trial, because when he has stood the test, he will receive the crown of life that God has promised to those who love him.
>
> (James 1:12)

Scripture declares that if we chase after the things of this world, we will be disappointed. Our lives will be taken away from us, and all we have built them on will crumble and fade away. A focus on the here and now prevents godly wisdom being manifested in our lives.

One of the TV programs I enjoy is *Antiques Roadshow*. In one episode a well-to-do lady came up to the jewelry specialist and, full of confidence, presented her with a beautiful gold and diamond ring. She told her that the ring had been in the family for centuries, handed down from generation to generation. The specialist took the ring, put a magnifying glass to her eye, and examined the stones. After a few moments of muttering under her breath she let out a loud "Oh dear!" She looked the well-to-do lady in the eye and said, "I'm terribly sorry, but this diamond ring is not a diamond ring at all: in fact the stones are made of glass. I'm afraid the only value this ring has is sentimental value." The lady's face was a real picture as she was told that her pride and joy, her "precious" treasure, was worth nothing!

Similarly, it would be terrible to stand before the Lord Jesus on judgment day, empty-handed because we have put our hope in the things of this world instead of in Him. We would find our treasure here on earth is worthless, and our hope in the things of this world is in vain.

Yet there is joy, hope, absolute and everlasting security through faith, found only in the mighty salvation that Jesus brings into our lives. Jesus has come to bring us the priceless gift of life, and life in all its abundance. We experience the first-fruits of this eternal treasure here on earth, but we see the full glory and reward when we see our Savior Jesus Christ in heaven. Jesus Himself calls us to invest our lives, energy, hope and trust in a treasure that does not fade or waste away, a treasure that lasts forever! Jesus says: "Store up for yourselves treasures in heaven, where moth and rust do not destroy, and where thieves do not break in and steal. For where your treasure is, there your heart will be also" (Matthew 6:20–21).

Psalm 37:18 declares the reality of plenty for those who trust in the Lord:

> The days of the blameless are known to the LORD,
>   and their inheritance will endure for ever.

Proverbs 10:22 encourages us to build our lives on the eternal wisdom of the Lord:

> The blessing of the LORD brings wealth,
>   and he adds no trouble to it.

We store up for ourselves treasure in heaven by forsaking the false securities of this world, and putting our faith in the salvation of Jesus. Acts 4:12 tells us:

> Salvation is found in no-one else [but Jesus], for there is no other name under heaven given to men by which by which we must be saved.

Only in Jesus is there forgiveness of sins. Only in Jesus is there new life. Only in Jesus is there a relationship with the God who created us. Only in Jesus is there life everlasting, and entrance into heaven.

As Christians we must not be seduced into focusing on, and trusting in, the things of this world. As children of God we should already know in our hearts where our security is. Our names are written in the Lamb's Book of Life, and Jesus has been preparing a place for us in heaven for the last two thousand years. By accepting the teaching of Scripture we should know the fullness of our reward, the fullness of our treasure, the fullness of the salvation waiting for us when we leave this life behind and enter into heaven's joy and delight. We should not chase after the things of this world, or invest our hope in them.

We need to keep our eyes and hearts firmly on Jesus, because those who belong to the Lord Jesus have been born again of "imperishable seed." In Colossians 3:1–3 we are encouraged as children of God to fix our minds on eternal things, on all that we have in Jesus, and to allow that living wisdom to improve our understanding. Scripture says that by binding ourselves to Jesus in faith, we have been united with Him in His death and resurrection. We have experienced a death of the sinful nature, and a spiritual resurrection that will ultimately result in a bodily resurrection. As people who live in resurrection power and hope, we are called to fix our eyes on the resurrected Christ who is seated at the right hand of the Father.

It is in Jesus that we have our reward and our inheritance. It is in Jesus that we are raised from the dead and given a body like His, fit for the conditions of eternity. As we focus on Jesus we understand that this life is not all that we have. In Him we have been included in a great salvation mystery whereby the Lord our God has made us His eternal children. We see that throughout Scripture the Lord has been looking for a people who will belong to Him. The Lord is looking for a people who will love Him, worship Him, obey His precepts, and fulfill His purposes here on earth. Through Jesus, the Lord Almighty has called people from every tribe and nation under heaven to come to Him, and by faith to receive the Spirit of adoption, the Spirit of sonship. When this happens by faith in Jesus, we are set free by all that Jesus has done for us – set free not only while we are on earth, but eternally.

We will never live sacrificial lives for Jesus until we understand our eternal inheritance in Him. We will never live free from anxiety until we accept that in Jesus our future is secure forever. Many Christian martyrs have endured unimaginable hardship, even death, with joy and hope because they had an unshakable belief in eternity with Jesus. They may have had nothing on this earth, and even what little they had was taken from them, but they endured suffering for the sake of Christ as a great privilege. They knew that what they shared in Christ in suffering would be transformed into a shared glory with Him in the life to come. Our minds must be renewed from temporary worries, with a solid foundation of trust and expectation in the Lord, a conviction that what He has promised will be. As Scripture says, we can gain the whole world, secure our lives with every mechanism of man, and yet forfeit our souls.

The hope that we have in Jesus can change us, setting us free to live lives focused on our absolute and permanent faith in Jesus. I love the fact that the Lord Jesus has set me free from the fears and anxieties of this world. He has set me free from chasing after the world's desires in a vain hope of securing my life. For in Jesus I have been given an inheritance that will not fade or pass away, an inheritance that is kept in heaven for me until the day I appear before the Eternal Lamb, the Lord Jesus Himself, when He will give me the crown of life.

There is nothing this world can do permanently to those who truly have their hearts and minds fixed on Jesus. As Paul says, describing his living testimony and simple focus: "to live is Christ and to die is gain" (Philippians 1:21). We are to be about Kingdom living and Kingdom-building while we are on this earth. We are here to live out the purposes of God, to spend our inheritance of life in service to the One who has created us, and saved us through Jesus. As I live my life in Jesus, whatever I face, the Lord is by my side. He is there as my comfort and my guide. He is the One who strengthens and empowers me to be and do all that He requires of me. Even if I am mocked or persecuted or things in this world go against me, as I am faithful to Him, He will be faithful to me. Even if my life is required of me, because I am united with Jesus through His death and resurrection I have the promise of resurrection and eternal life.

We need the Holy Spirit to educate our hearts to the wonderful, unfading glory of who we are and what we have in Jesus. The people of this world are building their lives and futures on shifting sand, but we are building our lives on the cornerstone, the capstone, Christ, the rock of our salvation that will not be shaken or eroded by the worst storms that this world can inflict on us. Our future in Him is secure and guaranteed. God, our heavenly Father, is the Alpha and Omega, the beginning and the end. He has always existed, and will always exist. He was there at the formation of the universe, and Scripture declares that all creation was created by Him and for Him. He is before all things and in Him all things have their existence. All power and authority in heaven and on earth are His, and when He makes a promise it is certain. When He opens a door, no man can close it. When He establishes something in eternity, for eternity it is established. To truly find the wisdom of God, to live in the power and freedom of that wisdom, we need to recognize that this world is passing away, but what we have in Jesus lasts forever.

When we look at the teaching of Scripture about becoming secure in the Lord, we see that it takes both a clear focus on the salvation of the Lord, and a simple persevering trust in His promises. Isaiah 26:3–4 says:

> You will keep in perfect peace
> > him whose mind is steadfast,
> > because he trusts in you.
> Trust in the Lord for ever,
> > for the Lord, the Lord, is the Rock eternal.

Scripture declares that there is a real and permanent peace for those who are in the Lord, but the security of that peace is found only by those who put their full trust in Him. Right now I can speak to my heart and my will, and say: "Today is a day when I will put my full trust in the Lord." As I read the Bible and understand it more fully, I can commit my mind and heart to trust the Word of God. I can sprinkle my faith on the revealed truth of the Lord. As I do this I am co-operating with the Holy Spirit to build an oasis of truth that will set my heart, mind and spirit free as I serve the Lord each day of my life. No longer bogged down by the worries of this world, I begin to find myself living and proving the promises of God in my daily life.

On many occasions Paul prayed for the Christians of his time to understand what is eternal, so that they might rejoice freely in Jesus. Eternal things are only spiritually discerned. We can understand the words written on the page, and grasp concepts that are explained to us. But for words to really have the power to change us, we need a living revelation bringing those words to life. We need to experience the full weight and glory of those words as we discover through them the unchanging reality of the Lord, breaking into human experience and enhancing it. As Paul put it in Ephesians 1:17–19:

> ... that the God of our Lord Jesus Christ, the Father of glory, may give to you the spirit of wisdom and revelation in the knowledge of Him, the eyes of your understanding may be enlightened; that you may know what is the hope of His calling, what are the riches of the glory of His inheritance in the saints, and what is the exceeding greatness of His power toward us who believe, according to the working of His mighty power.
>
> (NKJV)

The choice is simple for us, as God's people who love and follow His ways. We can fix our minds on what is temporary or on what is eternal; on the wisdom of man that does not last or on the unchanging reality of the Lord. Building our lives on the Lord is not just about hearing the eternal truths of the Lord, but also putting them into practice. In Matthew 7:24 Jesus emphasizes that it is not those who hear His words, but those who obey them, who will build their lives on the unshakable rock of His truth. Is it possible that we can train our minds in the reality of eternity? Is it possible for us as God's people to fix our eyes on the prize, the goal of our salvation? The hope of worldly glory inspires an athlete to great sacrifices of training and diet. How much more should the eternal glory that we share in Christ spur us on in our worship, service and witness to the Lord? When we understand the temporary nature of all that is around us, we begin to understand that we are in this world but not of it. When we see that any plan we make for ourselves is temporary, but the plans the Lord has for us last forever, then we can trust Him for those plans and encourage them to come to fruition. It is not that we are prohibited from enjoying our lives, or valuing wholesome temporary experiences, but that we should refuse to put our hope and trust in that which does not last. We should not try to secure our lives in that which will ultimately pass away.

This may be acceptable to people of the world, who have no other certainty. But for us who are united with Jesus there is a higher destiny, a fuller calling, and an eternal dwelling-place in that which is to come. In his letter to the Philippians Paul warns Christians against fixing their minds on earthly things. Those who do focus their lives on the things of this world will not inherit the Kingdom of Heaven:

> Their destiny is destruction, their god is their stomach, and their glory is in their shame. Their mind is on earthly things.
>
> (Philippians 3:19)

If our greatest delight is in the things of this world, the false glory that this world has to offer, then we will not be prepared to truly forsake all for the wonder of knowing Jesus. Paul saw that all he had going for him before he came to know Jesus was "rubbish" compared to the richness of grace, forgiveness and love found through Him. Rather than boasting of all he had achieved before he was saved, Paul declares that there is nothing in this entire world that compares with knowing Jesus.

Many people live in fear, anxious about the future, terrified of death. Jesus' coming into this world has the potential to set us free from these old ways of thinking and feeling. Jesus has destroyed death, and all the works of the evil one. He has conquered this world and all that was against us. That battle is won, our freedom has been secured, but we as Christians need to train our minds in this victory, equip ourselves for this freedom. We need to protect our hearts in the knowledge of what the Lord has secured in the present and the future for His people. We need to adjust our minds to the truth so that they are guarded by the "peace that passes all understanding." Jesus is the focus of this transformation from the old to the new. Jesus is the center of this revolution of the mind that takes our focus from the temporary to the eternal. As we worship Him in spirit and in truth, read His Word with open hearts, and seek His face and will in prayer, we realize that He is the one who reveals the awesome mystery that is our salvation. He is the one who gives us full understanding of the once-for-all, full and complete victory found in His death and resurrection, in the shedding of His blood and the gift of His Holy Spirit.

Trusting in what we have been given forever in Jesus transforms us from limited people focused on the now, to people of freedom who are seasoned in the eternal, and truly overcomers of this world. As Romans 8:37–39 says:

> ... we are more than conquerors through him who loved us. For I am convinced that neither death nor life, neither angels nor demons, neither the present nor the future, nor any powers, neither height nor depth, nor anything else in all creation, will be able to separate us from the love of God that is in Christ Jesus our Lord.

Chapter 6

The FEAR *of the* LORD

The fear of the LORD is the beginning of wisdom;
all who follow his precepts have good understanding.
To him belongs eternal praise.
(Psalm 111:10)

Many people's biggest struggle is with fear of what is out there in the world. Given the current state of humanity, it is not surprising that we are bombarded with anxiety about so many things: fear about what the future will hold, not only for ourselves but for our children and their children. Scientists predict a hundred different ways that the world will come to an end. Hollywood picks up on the theme and gives us disaster blockbusters depicting the world on the edge of destruction. Politicians use our fears against us, pushing through policies that would be unpopular if it were not for the current level of threat and suspicion. Even television producers have recognized our fears, and created game shows where people confront their worst nightmares for the sake of "entertainment." There is no doubt that many in our society have hidden fears, and live lives of quiet anxiety and doubt.

However, not all fears are bad. Fear has the capacity to make us think twice about putting ourselves into a potentially dangerous situation. We act more carefully when we have a healthy respect for what could go wrong. It helps us prepare sensibly so that we do not take things for granted. This is the attitude that the Lord wants us to have, in our relationship with Himself. Renewing and transforming the mind involves learning to fear the Lord. In Proverbs 1:7 we see "fear" at the heart of godly wisdom released into the lives of His people: "The fear of the Lord is the beginning of knowledge." The Hebrew word for "fear" here is *yirah*. Its root is *yare*, which means "to fear, be afraid, become frightened, fearful, showing reverence." Proverbs 2:5 confirms this:

> then you will understand the fear of the Lord
> and find the knowledge of God.

Throughout the book of Proverbs we see this continuing theme of learning to fear the Lord. We are told that fearing the Lord is the doorway to discovering godly wisdom and understanding for our lives.

If we fear the Lord, we grow in our sense of awe and respect towards Him, the One who is the Creator and maker of all. The result is that we learn to trust and obey Him in the things that He calls us to do. The fruit of this is that we establish our lives by obedience to His commands, thus releasing His wisdom into our lives. Fearing the Lord enables us to approach the One who created us and sustains by His mighty power. This makes us careful in approaching Him and living before Him, as we appreciate His absolute power and authority over our lives.

In Deuteronomy 4:10 we see how the giving of the law was to establish this godly fear in the lives of those who followed the Lord, so that they might be obedient to Him in loving service:

> "... especially concerning the day you stood before the Lord your God in Horeb, when the Lord said to me, 'Gather the people to Me, and I will let them hear My words, that they

may learn to fear Me all the days they live on the earth, and that they may teach their children.' "

(NKJV)

Here the Lord Himself is looking for us, His people, to have a healthy fear of Him, to stand in awe, to respect who He is and therefore what He can do. We gain a sense of wonder at His love, and awe at His grace. I believe that the church in many parts of the world has become too flippant before the Lord. We have lost our fear of the Lord of lords and King of kings, the One who holds our lives in His hands. We have lost the sense of His absolute sovereignty and power. So much of what goes on within the church is superficial and showy, instead of reverent and respectful to the Lord. Yes, there should be joy in our meetings, for we all know that there is celebration before the throne of the Lamb in heaven. However, our gatherings should center on giving the Lord Jesus the glory, honor, praise and adoration that He deserves, rather than entertaining or pleasing ourselves.

When we gather together to worship, we do so to minister unto Him what He desires and deserves. Despite some of our circumstances, the Lord does not change: more importantly, His glory does not change, His nature and ways do not change. Therefore He is always worthy of our love, our praise, our adoration. Scripture makes it clear that none of us will see the true wisdom of God manifested in our lives, unless we learn to fear the Lord and respect His sovereign hand over our lives. None of us can have a renewed mind to test and affirm the Lord's perfect will, unless we understand how to stand in awe before Him. He is not our buddy buddy! He is the Lord Almighty, He is our God and King. We should make sure that we do not overstep the mark or take liberties with Him.

In Psalm 34:1–22 David challenges us with the importance of fearing God. It is through David's great fear and respect for God that His intimacy with God is cultivated. The fear of the Lord caused David to seek after Him with all his heart, and trust in

God alone for his provision. At this point David is desperate, even in peril for his life. He has fled his own country due to Saul and his death threats, and found himself in the land of his enemies. In 1 Samuel 21:10–14 the king brings David before him. He is in fear for his life, so pretends to be mad. The king believes him and lets him go. It is in the midst of all this insecurity, with death threats, wandering around banished from his own land, that David writes this psalm. The fear of the Lord results in worship of Him, even in the most difficult situation.

He starts the psalm with a few verses of wonderful praise. For David, fear of the Lord has emerged from contemplation of His awesome, mighty and powerful nature. Perceiving God in this way, David's spirit is lifted up to praise the Lord for who He is. David has begun to understand what a mighty God he has, and he is stirred to give the Lord the glory He deserves. This is important to us, because what we see here is praise and honor of the Lord that transcends a person's circumstances and enables them to worship the Lord, whatever the circumstances of their life:

> I will extol the LORD *at all times*;
>> his praise will always be on my lips.
> My soul will boast in the LORD;
>> let the afflicted hear and rejoice.
> Glorify the LORD with me:
>> let us exalt his name together.
>
> (Psalm 34:1–3, emphasis added)

To come to a consistent level of wisdom and assurance we need to understand, like David, that whatever we go through the Lord is sovereign and rules over all. Here is spontaneous praise in the context of serious suffering. David has done nothing wrong, but even in fear of his life he is faithful to God. Yet he is still suffering persecution.

Why, in the midst of his problems, can David worship God with such simple beauty? *The reason is that he fears the Lord.*

Likewise, when we truly fear the Lord, whatever we go through in this world loses the sting of terror. David understands that the Lord is faithful, that He holds the nations of this world in the palm of His hand. Because he has attained a reverent awe for the Lord, he knows that nothing can harm him while the Lord governs his life. It may seem strange that one fear has the power to cast out all other fears, but this is the truth presented in Scripture. Verse 4 shows that the Lord has delivered David from all his fears:

> I sought the LORD, and he answered me;
> he delivered me from *all my fears*
>
> (emphasis added)

When we see the vastness of the Lord, the tenderness and love He has for His children, then His perfect loves casts out all our fears, for we know that He is the one who governs our lives. Why has David been delivered from all his earthly fears? We find the answer in verse 7:

> The angel of the LORD encamps around those who fear him,
> and he delivers them.

David understands the ability of the Lord to keep, protect and aid His people. There may be suffering for a while, but David believes that the Lord will sustain those who belong to Him. As he goes through the trying times he sees the Lord's angel sent to minister to him, to guide him to a place of safety.

Just like David, when we go through times of trial the question is how we respond. Like David, we have a choice. We can turn our backs on the Lord and blame Him for our circumstances; we can doubt His goodness; we can accuse Him of not caring for us. At certain times in their lives many Christians do choose to respond in these ways, but such responses will not bring about the long-term plan of the Lord. It will not give us peace and hope while we travel through the wilderness to a place of good pasture again. Or, like David, we can worship the Lord in every situation with all of our hearts. We can recognize that the Lord does not change, that His goodness and love do not change. We can see the many blessings He has to give us, and know that He is Almighty God, worthy of our praise whatever our circumstances. David's testimony is that if we fear the Lord and live a life worthy of Him, then the Lord provides for His people. We see a God who frees us from fears even before we receive our deliverance.

We are called to us to stand in awe of the Lord Almighty:

> Fear the LORD, you his saints,
>   for those who fear him lack nothing.
> The lions may grow weak and hungry,
>   but those who seek the LORD lack no good thing.
>
>   (Psalm 34:9–10)

When we approach the Lord in a worthy way and acknowledge who He is, the promise of Scripture is that we will *lack no good thing*. Jesus Himself made it clear that if we keep the Lord at the forefront of our minds and live in obedience to the Kingdom, then the Lord will add all we need to our lives. Instead of chasing after the supposed securities of this world we are encouraged to fear the Lord, to live our lives in line with His Kingdom. God will meet all our needs. From our fear of the Lord, and our intimacy with Him, we are called to live lives worthy of Him, trusting in His goodness:

> The eyes of the LORD are on the righteous
>   and his ears are attentive to their cry.
>
>   (Psalm 34:15)

Many will say that surely love, rather than fear, is a better reason to live a life worthy of the Lord. Surely love is a greater motivator for us to please the Lord by the way that we live and the closeness that we cultivate with Him. But love of the Lord and fear of the Lord are not opposed to each other, and not mutually exclusive. David was called a man after God's own heart, a man who loved the Lord with all his heart. He was not perfect, in fact he committed some serious sins against the Lord, yet he loved and served the Lord with a passion. David had encountered the Lord's sovereignty and power. He had seen the Lord's mighty right arm, and been humbled before his God. Both love and fear of the Lord characterized David's life.

The sad fact about the church today is that we teach the love of the Lord and the mercy of the Lord, but we have forsaken the sovereignty, majesty and fear of the Lord. As a result we are in danger of creating people who accept the Lord's love and blessing, but will not accept His discipline and refinement: people who will follow the Lord in the good times, but will abandon Him when the going gets tough. David feels the weight of his problems, yet shows a powerful faith in the nature of God. He believes that even though God has not delivered him fully yet, it will happen.

This is the type of faith that Jesus is looking for within you and me, a faith that simply trusts in the nature of our Lord. He is looking for a commitment to Him that believes in His deliverance, His provision, His healing, while these processes are taking place. This is a strong faith that believes in the goodness of God even when the circumstances don't seem to change. It is this type of faith that shapes situations for the glory of God, a faith released through revelation of the power and authority of God over His creation. This brings the fear of the Lord in such a way that we trust Him, in His might, to deliver and establish His Kingdom amongst the people of today's world. It brings a fear of the Lord that produces love and trust, along with awe and respect for His true nature.

But we in the church are in danger of undermining a clear spiritual truth, a truth we ignore at our peril. Modern Christian culture wants to do away with the fear of the Lord. It is frowned upon to preach of a Holy God and the reality of judgment, hell and damnation, as preachers did in the past. Many Christian books persuade us that to build the church we need to preach only on the grace and love of God. We are told to avoid anything that will offend people or cause them to fear the One who can cast them into hell. "Old Testament" subjects like holiness, justice or condemnation are frowned upon and seen as unfitting for the modern mind. The church is sweeping under the carpet the awesomeness and fearfulness of the Lord: this is unbiblical. We are told by church growth movements to avoid preaching that we are sinners, preaching about judgment, preaching about God's holiness – in fact, to avoid preaching anything that may be seen as offensive. We are in danger of establishing a counterfeit church that has more to do with the foolish wisdom of man than the righteous decrees of God. We are told to preach on His grace to meet our needs, His desire for all to go to heaven, His willingness to accept our failings and still love us as His children.

We are producing a breed of people who come to church to have their needs met and be entertained. They want a fake gospel that is not about the holiness and glory of Jesus, but about the "I" in our lives. We are producing a shallow "feel-goodism" that has no power to save, or to see people through the difficult times of their lives. When God's people lose the fear of the Lord they are in danger of creating a false God made in the image of man and catering to his selfish desires.

Scripture declares that the Lord is to be feared and respected. In the Old Testament He wiped out whole nations and armies that came against His people. He is the One who banished His people into exile when they were unfaithful to Him, who laid the full weight of your sin and mine upon His Son, who holds your life and mine in the palm of His hand. He is the one true God, creator of heaven and earth, who will judge all of humanity – sending some to eternal damnation and others to eternal life. This may be hard to accept, but it is the revealed truth of the Lord who calls us into relationship with Himself. We cannot create Him in our image, or avoid parts of the Old Testament to tone His actions down and make Him more comfortable. He is who He is, and nothing will change that. The Lord says about Himself: I AM WHO I AM (Exodus 3:14). The fear of the Lord is the beginning of all wisdom, for in our own eyes the Lord is exalted and lifted up and we are humbled in willing submission and obedience to Him. As Isaiah 33:6 says:

> He will be the sure foundation for your times,
>   a rich store of salvation and wisdom and knowledge;
>   the fear of the LORD is the key to this treasure.

This is Old Testament teaching with relevance to you and me who believe in Jesus, for even Jesus and the early disciples taught about fearing the Lord. You may have heard preachers say that as Christians we do not need to fear the Lord, because we are under grace. I would say yes, we are under grace, but that has not done away with the fear of the Lord. Here are the words of Jesus Himself, from Matthew 10:28:

> "Do not be afraid of those who kill the body, but cannot kill the soul. Rather, be afraid of the One who can destroy both soul and body in hell."

In 2 Corinthians 5:10–11 Paul describes living in fear of the Lord, and how that fear motivates him to witness to the whole world:

> For we must all appear before the judgment seat of Christ, that each one may receive what is due to him for the things done while in the body, whether good or bad. Since, then, we know what it is to fear the Lord, we try to persuade men.

In the letter to the Hebrews, written to Christians, the writer challenges us to persevere in a true profession of faith, for judgment is around the corner:

> If we deliberately keep on sinning after we have received the knowledge of the truth, no sacrifice for sins is left, but only a

fearful expectation of judgment and of raging fire that will
consume the enemies of God ... It is a dreadful thing to fall
into the hands of the living God.

(Hebrews 10:26, 31)

When we understand the purposes of God, and know that all
creation is accountable to Him, we become careful about how
we behave and live. The fear of the Lord is a healthy attitude,
because it is a sobering thought that there will be a day of
judgment, a day when all creation will stand before the throne
of the Lamb and give an account of how we have lived.

When we consider the holiness and sovereignty of the Lord,
we are compelled to be careful how we live. We seek to live
lives in line with His holiness, lives pleasing to Him. As we gaze
upon the Lord we recognize that He is perfectly moral, and is
displeased with His children when they sin against Him or each
other. The fear of the Lord, as well as love for the Lord,
compels us to do what is right and avoid what is wrong and
displeasing to God. In this way holiness from the Lord is
manifested in our lives. We are building our lives on the living
foundation of His truth, led by His Spirit. The thought that our
lives may be displeasing to the Lord should spur us on to walk
daily down that narrow path of righteousness – not to save us,
for we are saved in Christ, but to walk in wisdom so that our
lives truly honor the Lord in the eyes of others.

Now we know that through faith in Jesus we are part of Him,
and through His grace we are saved. However, there is still a
judgment of works that is due, even for Christians. Scripture
declares that some who belong to Christ will just scrape into
heaven with the smell of burning upon their clothes: all their
works will be burnt up by the testing of fire, but they will just
get into heaven by their profession of faith.

For me and for many Christians there is the wonderful joy
and confidence that we have in the Lord Jesus and the salvation
He has given us. However, there must be a great desire for our
lives to be worthy of Him, so that He will take pleasure in the

things we do for Him, and on that great day when we see our Savior face to face He will say to us, "Well done good and faithful servant, you have done what you have done for Me, and have done all that was asked of you."

Many Christians today talk about getting back to the principles of the early church, and building the church on the model of fellowship that the early church had. Yet it is rarely mentioned that the early church, despite the wonderful intimacy and power of the Holy Spirit, lived in fear of the Lord. Acts 9:31 gives us the testimony of those early Christians:

> Then the church throughout Judea, Galilee and Samaria enjoyed a time of peace. It was strengthened; and encouraged by the Holy Spirit, it grew in numbers, *living in the fear of the Lord.*
>
> (emphasis added)

If we are serious about growing in the mind of Christ, about being transformed by the renewing of our minds, then as David says we must learn the fear of the Lord. For to gain a mind renewed in the things of God, "The fear of the LORD is the beginning of all knowledge" (Proverbs 1:7).

Chapter 7

LAYING ALL
on the ALTAR

Then Jesus said to his disciples, "If anyone would come after me,
he must deny himself and take up his cross and follow me.
For whoever wants to save his life will lose it, but whoever
loses his life for me will find it. What good will it be for a man
if he gains the whole world, yet forfeits his soul?"
(Matthew 16:24–26)

In this chapter I want to establish a simple process for discerning and walking in the purposes of God for our lives. This process is the letting go of our ambitions and desires, and learning to discern and obey the perfect will of God for our lives. Renewing the mind means having the courage to lay before the Lord every plan that we have for our lives, and allowing Him to lead us down His secure pathway for our future.

In Matthew 16 Jesus declares that if anyone is going to follow Him they must deny self, take up their cross and follow Him. It is not popular today to talk about denying ourselves anything. In the eyes of many Christians, church has become a consumer product that we can take or leave, depending on whether it meets our needs or enriches us in the way we want. With emerging church models encouraging strange experiences, and "prosperity theology" defining our rights as Christians, to talk about denying ourselves anything seems old-fashioned and out of touch with the modern world. However, there is only one Gospel, where Jesus made it clear that we as His people are called to live lives that are in active obedience – not to our wills or our rights, but to the plans and the purposes of God. The problem is very clear: if I have already defined what my future holds, what I will and will not do, then I am not open to God's plans for my life. In fact if I have my "ten-year-plan" I am not going to listen to what the Holy Spirit may say, in case He contradicts what I have already decided for myself! With a preconceived plan for my life, I am limited in how I can listen, discern and respond to God's guidance. I will stand or fall, even as a Christian, by my own best guesses and efforts, and I am asking God to bless the plans I have already made for my life.

Making our own plans and defining our own destiny is not Christian, and will not in the long term bless our lives as people of God. As Christians we walk in the footsteps of our Savior. We follow His example and seek to live our lives in such a way that our hearts and minds respond to the different circumstances we find ourselves in, as the Lord Himself did. To know whether we should live our lives for ourselves or for the Lord, we only need look at the example of Jesus. He made it clear that He did not come to do His own will, but the will of Him who sent Him. The deeds that Jesus did, and the experiences that He endured, were directed by the desires of God for His life. Jesus made it clear that His whole life was given in service to fulfill the purposes that the Father had ordained. His very reason for coming into the world was to complete that which the Father had planned for Him:

> "For I have come down from heaven not to do my will but to do the will of him who sent me."
>
> (John 6:38)

Clearly, whatever was in the heart and mind of Jesus as He lived the life of a real human being, His first and only desire was to do the work the Father had prepared for Him. He declared that doing the will of the Father was what sustained Him:

> "My food," said Jesus, "is to do the will of him who sent me and to finish his work."
>
> (John 4:34)

Jesus gives us a wonderful example of a heart completely faithful and obedient to the Father. Here is the Lord of lords, who created the heavens and the earth, not coming into the world to rule or demand His rights as Lord, but willingly submitting Himself to serve and give His life as a ransom to save the lost. This self-giving servant heart is what the Lord calls His people to follow. Matthew 20:25–28 makes it clear that we are not to exert our rights against each other, or expect special treatment when we feel we have "got somewhere" in Kingdom terms. In fact, Jesus made it clear that if we want to be great in the Kingdom of God, we must have a servant heart like His towards the Father:

> "You know that the rulers of the Gentiles lord it over them, and their high officials exercise authority over them. *Not so with you.* Instead, whoever wants to become great among you must be your servant, and whoever wants to be first must be your slave – just as the Son of Man did not come to be served, but to serve, and to give his life as a ransom for many."
>
> (emphasis added)

This statement of the Lord challenges us about how we hold on to our rights and our preferences in the face of others' needs. It challenges the worldly living of Christian superstars who buy personal jets and amass great fortunes at the expense of those who support their ministries. Jesus was perfect in every way, and at the heart of His perfection was obedience to the plans of God. As Philippians 2:5–11 puts it:

Your attitude should be the same as that of Christ Jesus:

> ... he humbled himself
> and became obedient to death – even death on a cross!
> Therefore God exalted him to the highest place
> and gave him the name that is above every name ...
>
> (verses 5, 8–9)

Not only did Jesus do the work that the Father had ordained for Him, He also made it clear that it was the task of all who follow Him to do the same. Jesus makes it clear that such obedience is a sign of someone who truly belongs to Him:

> "Not everyone who says to me, 'Lord, Lord,' will enter the kingdom of heaven, *but only he* who does the will of my Father who is in heaven."
>
> (Matthew 7:21, emphasis added)

> He replied to him, "Who is my mother, and who are my brothers?" Pointing to his disciples, he said, "Here are my mother and my brothers. For whoever does the will of my Father in heaven is my brother and sister and mother."
>
> (Matthew 12:48–50)

As followers of Jesus, we must know that just as the Lord came to do the will of the Father for His life, so we who follow Him are here to fulfill the plan of the Father for our lives. Even in the Garden of Gethsemane, where Jesus struggled humanly with the burden of all that He had to endure, the pain and humiliation and sin He had to carry, the cry of His heart was "not my will, but yours be done" (Luke 22:42). When we understand from Ephesians 2 that we are God's workmanship, created to do good works that the Lord has prepared in advance for us, we also need to be prepared in our daily lives to say, "Not my will, but Yours be done."

It was through this determination of the Lord Jesus to do the will of the Father that a mighty anointing of power through the

Holy Spirit was released on His life. Jesus was fully equipped as a human being to do the work of His Father in heaven. Likewise, when the Lord's people are about His business, the Lord is willing to equip us with power and wisdom to do that which is required of us. Such qualities were released into Jesus' life as He walked in step with the Holy Spirit. He could therefore heal the sick, calm storms, raise the dead, and overcome the opposition of demons and cynics. This all became possible as the Holy Spirit released anointing on Jesus to manifest the signs of the coming Kingdom.

The fundamental principle here is that divine guidance and power only become possible when we submit ourselves to the will of God. As a people who belong to the Lord, we should know that doing things our own way will not help us develop lives that are secure in the wisdom of Jesus. Doing things our own way will not release into our lives the full potential that we have in Jesus, as His full provision empowers His will in our lives. If we want to move in the wisdom and purposes of God then we must lay all on the altar. While we hold on to our own ambitions we have a focus that takes our eyes off God's plans. While we chase after the desires of our hearts we become blind to the direction of the Holy Spirit. This shuts us off from the practical guidance that the Lord offers us to build our lives on Him.

Once I was trying to carry two boxes downstairs. I put one on top of the other, lifted them up, and walked down the stairs. When I got to the room where I wanted to put the boxes, the door was shut. We all know that men are stubborn, so rather than putting the boxes down, I tried to tried to open the door with my elbow. After about five minutes of twisting and turning, the door still would not open, so I tried to use my knee. As I stretched up to rest my knee on the handle I overbalanced and fell sideways, dropping both boxes and spilling their contents on the floor. All I needed to do was to let go of the boxes, and my hands would have been free to open the door.

When our hands are full we cannot grasp hold of something new. This is true for us spiritually: while we hold on to the plans and ambitions of our own hearts, we find it hard to grasp hold of God's purposes for our lives. So often, in our own lives and in the life of the church, Christians have already made their own plans for what they want to happen, and we find it hard to be fully open to the Lord. We cannot let Him break into our lives, to have His say and have His way.

If we look at the fall of man in the Garden of Eden, or the fall of Lucifer, we see that pride comes before a fall. Adam and Eve followed their own agenda when the serpent told them they would be like God if they ate the fruit from the tree. They wanted self-determination, rejecting the perfect direction of the Lord and following their own desires. Lucifer followed his own agenda when he tried to direct all creation to worship himself. He wanted to be God himself. Again he chose the path of self-determination, and destroyed the perfection of God's created order. What a contrast we see between these two examples and the servant life of Jesus! When Jesus calls us to Himself, He calls us to the task of hearing and obeying God's purposes for our lives. He calls us to deny the plans and desires that would stand against the will of God. The challenge for us is to let go of self-determination, and walk the path of godly determination.

Real wisdom is developed in our lives as Kingdom people, when we put the interests of the Kingdom above any personal interests of our own. In Romans 12:1 we are called to be "living sacrifices, holy and pleasing to God." Because of all that Jesus has done for us, this is our reasonable response, our reasonable service to Him. We should be prepared to lay all before the throne of Jesus, allowing Him to give back to us what He wants for our lives. Taking up the cross is about sacrificing to the Lord the "I" in our lives, and putting Jesus at the center.

Whatever our society says about the rights of the individual to self-determination, we as Christians are called to reject self-centeredness for Christ-centeredness. When we do this we follow Jesus, fulfilling God's will for our lives through the power of the Holy Spirit. We cannot follow Jesus truly and live for self. We cannot live in the power of Jesus and pursue our own plans. When we truly follow Jesus we live for Jesus, each day of our earthly lives. When we give everything to Jesus to take and use as He sees fit, our minds become open to the purposes He has for us. All of us should take time regularly to give all the different areas of our lives to the Lord, and ask Him to direct them as He sees fit. It is a good discipline to submit to God our plans for our lives, families, careers, finances, homes, gifts, skills and callings, relationships and church life; and to ask the Lord to have His way for us in all these things. As Matthew 6:24 says:

> "No-one can serve two masters; either he will hate the one and love the other, or he will be devoted to the one and despise the other. You cannot serve both God and Money."

There is only room for one person on the throne of our lives. There is only room for one person to guide and govern the steps that we take. We cannot bow the knee to Jesus, and then ask Him to bow the knee to us in our choices and decisions for ourselves. Jesus warns us that we can do it our own way, we can get everything we want for our lives, but we will completely miss the great plan and reward of God for our lives. Following Jesus means going the whole journey with Him. He guides our footsteps, directs our path, shows us where we should place our feet. Jesus tells us "whoever desires to save his life will lose it, but whoever loses his life for My sake will find it" (Matthew 16:25 NKJV). True security as a follower of God comes by doing the works that the Lord has planned for our lives. We can buy the right house in the right location, get the right job, and achieve a position of authority. Yet if this is not the Lord's plan for our lives, gaining these things will in the long term lose us the inheritance that Jesus wants to give us:

"For what profit is it to a man, if he gains the whole world, and loses his own soul? Or what will a man give in exchange for his soul?"

(Matthew 16:26 NKJV)

We need to look at our lives, our dreams and our ambitions, and ask if there is anything we would exchange our soul for. Would we exchange it for money, fame, recognition, power, or for a particular dream to come true? Jesus tells us that we can gain our dreams and fulfill our plans, but lose what is really precious to us. Psalm 127 gives us important advice in this area:

Unless the LORD builds the house,
They labor in vain who build it;
Unless the LORD guards the city,
The watchman stays awake in vain.

(Psalm 127:1 NKJV)

A sacrifice, once it has been made, does not get off the altar by itself. The problem many of us have is that we are not consistent in laying all we have on the altar. We put something before the Lord, or even into His hands, but we let go of it one moment then snatch it back the next. If we are to follow Jesus, then we need to do the will of our Father in heaven. That means reaching the point in our own lives where we cry, "Lord, not my will, but Yours be done." Whatever the cost, whatever the inconvenience or risk, we must deny self, take up the cross of self-denial, and follow Jesus. On the day He returns He will reward each one of us according to the works we have done in His name. As Matthew 16:27 says:

"For the Son of Man is going to come in his Father's glory with his angels, and then he will reward each person according to what he has done."

To renew our minds in the wisdom of the Lord for daily living, we must *let go* and *let God*! There is an altar before the throne of grace for us on which to lay our lives and ambitions, as we trust the Lord with our future. Summarizing the scriptures we have been considering in this chapter, He declares to us:

I will direct your paths and bring you into a land that is plentiful where you will find rest.

Chapter 8

RENEWED *by* TRUTH

Blessed is the man
who does not walk in the counsel of the wicked
or stand in the way of sinners
or sit in the seat of mockers.
But his delight is in the law of the LORD,
and on his law he meditates day and night.
He is like a tree planted by streams of water,
which yields its fruit in season
and whose leaf does not wither.
Whatever he does prospers.
(Psalm 1:1–3)

To renew our minds, we must respond to the Word of God. So far in this book, we have described practical pathways to follow every day in developing as Christians. This may seem difficult or strange at first because our minds have been shaped by a worldly perspective, but as we seek godly things we are led down pathways of wisdom. Practical requirements include: what influences us; setting our minds on what lasts forever; cultivating a fear of the Lord; and learning to lay all on the altar. All these have real power, if we persevere with them, to release in us the mind of Christ. Perhaps as you read this book you ask yourself, "How on earth do I reprogram my mind so that the rubbish of this world is filtered out? How do I live in the wisdom of the Lord? How do I move in the flow of God's wisdom so that His promises are daily realities in my life? How do I live out His plan for me?"

The answers are manifested in Scripture. Psalm 1 calls us to cultivate renewed minds in Christ, and tells us how our minds can be renewed. The question is not "Can our minds be renewed?", for nothing is impossible with the Lord, but rather "Are we prepared to follow God's ordained process so that this renewal will take place?" The renewal process is described in Psalm 1:2:

> But his delight is in the law of the LORD,
> and on his law he meditates day and night.

If we want to be blessed in our lives, if we want our lives to prosper in a godly way, then we must love the Word of God and take time to read and digest God's words of wisdom for our lives. Knowing, learning and applying Scripture to our lives is the fundamental way to grow in the thoughts of God. Without the foundation of Scripture to guide us, our lives are built on the shifting sand of our own desire and understanding. We hear sermons about reading the Word. We are encouraged at house groups and meetings with our pastor to read the Bible more. But still, few of the people of God do so on a regular basis.

One excuse I have heard a number of times is: "Well, I don't understand everything that the Word is saying to me." While I sympathize with this response, it should not be a reason to give up learning from the Word of the Lord. With such an abundance of Bible notes, study Bibles, Bibles in our native language, and Bible commentaries, there is no excuse for the Lord's people not to read His Word and build their lives on His commands. You cannot live your life in line with God's will, unless you feed daily on the Word of God. You cannot rely on your own thoughts and inclinations of the heart to make godly daily choices, unless you really know God's will from His Word.

God's Word, when taken into our minds and memorized, actually forms channels of thinking which bring revelations of God's active will. The seeds of God's Word shape our thoughts, leading us into the wisdom of God for our life-situations. In the church that I pastor we have talked a lot about Bible memorization, and I would say to all God's people that if we are serious about knowing the mind of Christ then we need to learn God's Word. It becomes an oasis of truth that the Holy Spirit uses to make our witness for God effective.

When we consider education, we see that people go to university to train their minds in particular disciplines that will give them understanding to do a particular job. How many of us would let someone do brain surgery on us, unless they had completed medical training? How many of us would get on an airplane with a pilot who had not learned to fly? Learned knowledge gives people the expertise to do a particular job. The Christian life is no different. If we are to move in the wisdom of the Lord, if we are to be Christ's ambassadors here on earth, and witness to His salvation, then we need to educate ourselves in the living textbook of the Christian faith. Knowledge of God's Word gives us the understanding of the Lord we need to make proper choices.

We can use Psalm 1 to cultivate our minds, helping us to grow as a man or woman of God. We find in this psalm that we must reject any thoughts that might lead us into sin or promote doubt in God's Word. Verse 1 states:

> Blessed is the man
> Who walks not in the counsel of the ungodly,
> Nor stands in the path of sinners,
> Nor sits in the seat of the scornful [or the mocker].
>
> (NKJV)

The psalmist is talking about the ideas and patterns of the world. As we saw in chapter 4, what we take into our minds has an effect on us. If we get involved with films, books or people that promote godless morality, then we will be influenced. There is a "law of association." What and who we associate with, we become like. Many Christians have started their Christian lives well, have grown spiritually and manifested a deep passion for Jesus, but over time have mixed with more worldly Christians – and have eventually made compromises with morality and truth.

I recently saw the film *Super Size Me,* a documentary about an American – Morgan Spurlock – who decided to conduct a personal experiment with fast food. For several months he ate only at McDonald's. For breakfast, dinner and tea, all he ate was McDonald's. This may seem like heaven to young people, but it was fascinating and shocking to see the effect of this fast food diet on his life. He put on a lot of weight, his cholesterol level went sky-high, and his blood pressure shot up. The food produced addictive cravings, and his emotions see-sawed up and down. Doctors finally warned him that if he continued with his fast food diet, he would do irreversible damage to his bodily health. This provides a simple warning to us as Christians. We can see ourselves as people of this world, do the same things as those around us, and allow this sinful society to shape us. But eventually these habits will make us unhealthy and flabby in our faith. Ephesians 4:22–24, written to Christians, warns us not to continue in the corrupted and deceitful patterns of the past:

> You were taught, with regard to your former way of life, to put off your old self, which is being corrupted by its deceitful desires, to be *made new in the attitude of your minds*; and to put on the new self, created to be like God in true righteousness and holiness.
>
> (emphasis added)

To put off the old self and put on the new self is a choice that we make each day. We should reject the influences of the world, and cultivate the qualities we find in Jesus. Perhaps the church in this country needs to be a kind of spiritual *Weight Watchers*! We should teach Christians the habits of discipleship, help them to change sinful patterns of behavior, and show them how to feed on the nourishing goodness of God's Word. In Joshua 1, Joshua is told by the Lord that he will lead the people to inherit the land that He has promised them. One condition for Joshua's success is to obey the Word of the Lord. He must read the Word, and meditate on it day and night so that it becomes part of him. The Word must inform his choices. The truth of the Lord will be a hedge to Joshua's left and right, guiding him along the pathway directed by the Lord. As Joshua steps out in courage, he is told that the Lord God is with him wherever he goes:

> Be strong and very courageous. Be careful to obey all the law my servant Moses gave you; do not turn from it to the right or to the left, that you may be successful wherever you go. Do not let this Book of the Law depart from your mouth; meditate on it day and night, so that you may be careful to do everything written in it. Then you will be prosperous and successful.
>
> (Joshua 1:7–8)

While obeying God's Word, we need to avoid Christians who are cynical towards it, who mock the simple faith of those who believe the Word. It is fashionable for self-proclaimed Christian "intellectuals" to undermine or dilute the Word of God. These self-appointed theologians apparently want to dismantle every Bible-based moral principle accepted by the church for the last two thousand years. The revealed truth of Scripture has always had academic critics and doubters, but this Christian generation like no other seems to believe what faithless teachers have to say. So many followers of Jesus doubt His words to us, His people. They read the Word of the Lord, and in their hearts they say cynically: "Yeah, right, that's really going to happen!"

Scripture declares that mockery of God's truth is a sin. It

produces a weak and compromised faith. It is no surprise, in a generation where our church leaders and theologians are continually undermining the authority of Scripture, that very few churches are moving in the power of Jesus. Sadly we are a generation that loves to mock the Word of God, and we do not acknowledge His spiritual truth. It seems that everything beyond the human mind is rejected.

We must put aside the dismissive attitudes and sinful patterns of this world, and free our hearts to learn from the Word of God. We need to go back to the simple truth that all Scripture is inspired by God, and is the final authority on *all matters* pertaining to faith, life and practice. Its authority should define our thinking and actions. There are questions to be asked about our relationship with Scripture, and its effect on our lives. Think about the Word of God that we can read in our own language. Do we love it? Do we, as Psalm 1 says, delight in reading its revelations? Do we spend time not just skimming over the surface of the Word, but stripping it back, reading it over and over again, asking questions of what it says until we understand it? Do we let its goodness seep into our minds and souls as we submit to its authority? Do we allow its truth to move our hearts to obedience? For when we do these things then we become a blessed and prosperous people in the things of the Kingdom. Psalm 1 promises that those who meditate on the Word day and night become like fruitful trees, bringing forth the fruit of godly living for the glory of God. It is a prosperity that does not wither as our lives change, but secures us in a place of God's will, enriched by His grace. The Word brings godly prosperity in all that we do for His name. Verse 3 of the psalm says that those who chew, digest and obey God's word are "like a tree planted by streams of water."

Jesus declared that He wanted us to bear much fruit, thereby showing ourselves to be His disciples. The nourishment of the Word produces growth in us as followers of Jesus. And the Lord keeps His word to us. If He wants us to bear Kingdom fruit in our lives, He will provide for it. In John 15 Jesus declares Himself to be the true vine in whom we are rooted and nourished. Jesus makes it clear that if we appear to be united with Him but do not produce the fruit of godly living, then the Father will cut off each unfruitful branch and throw it into the fire. Jesus wants us to bear not just a thirty-fold or sixty-fold harvest, in our lives as His people: because of the good seed of the Gospel sown in our lives, He expects a hundred-fold harvest from us, for the honor and glory of Himself. It should be the norm, not the exception, for us as Christians to be mightily fruitful for the Lord.

The joy of Kingdom living is this: if we build our lives on the Word of the Lord, then year by year we see an increase in the fruit of godly living as children of God. Rather than expecting new Christians to settle down and become like us, we should be expecting – both for them and ourselves – to greatly increase our fruitfulness, our passion, our service, our ministry and our obedience to the Lord Jesus. The Word of God is a wonderful blessing in our lives, an instrument that will transform our minds and understanding. It has been given us to cultivate channels of godly wisdom that will direct our choices each day. It has been given as a source of discernment so that we can live lives pleasing to the Lord.

A wonderful passage of Scripture, showing us the power of God's words to change us, is Psalm 119. Listen to some of its verses, and sense the power of God's Word to release God's people into godly living:

> How can a young man keep his way pure?
> 　By living according to your word.
>
> (verse 9)

> Turn my eyes away from worthless things;
> 　preserve my life according to your word.
>
> (verse 37)

> Teach me knowledge and good judgment,
> 　for I believe in your commands.
>
> (verse 66)

Oh, how I love your law!
  I meditate on it all day long.
Your commands make me wiser than my enemies,
  for they are ever with me.
I have more insight than all my teachers,
  for I meditate on your statutes.

(verses 97–99)

It is not a matter of luck whether we become anointed as Christians or not. Meditating on the Word of the Lord releases the deep wisdom of God into our lives so that we can oppose those who are against us, and even teach the teachers the things of the Kingdom. To love and obey God's Word is the divinely appointed way for us to become wise in the things of the Kingdom. If we do not cultivate these things in our lives then we will never be fruitful in the things of God. 2 Timothy 3:16–17 declares:

> *All* Scripture is God-breathed and is useful for teaching, rebuking, correcting and training in righteousness, *so that the man of God may be thoroughly equipped for every good work.*
>
> (emphasis added)

Scripture makes it clear that if we want to live lives worthy of Jesus, to understand God's revelation, to be equipped for every opportunity that God has for us, then we need to meditate on the Scripture of the Lord. It is by the Word that we know what is sinful, that we know God's direction for every situation of our lives, that we understand the nature of God and His actions. As Christians we have a choice. Yes, we can act by gut instinct, or by an uncertain spiritual revelation, but every prompting of our hearts and minds has to be submitted to the test of Scripture to reveal its origin.

The Word of God can make us wise in our salvation and discerning towards God, not only for our own lives but for the lives of others. The Word has power to rewrite our morals, beliefs and desires so that godly wisdom is manifested in our lives. If we are serious about walking in the wisdom of God for our lives, about prospering in all that we do in line with the Lord's will, then we need to allow the Word of God to renew our minds. We need to read, learn, memorize and be nourished by God's words of living truth and revelation. As Psalm 1:3 says:

> He is like a tree planted by streams of water,
>   which yields its fruit in season
> and whose leaf does not wither.
>   Whatever he does prospers.

Chapter 9

The
HOLY SPIRIT
OUR TEACHER

*But the wisdom that comes from heaven is first of all pure;
then peace-loving, considerate, submissive, full of mercy and
good fruit, impartial and sincere.*
(James 3:17)

When we consider the wisdom of the Lord, we see it as a generous gift of the Lord, which He releases within us when we follow His prescribed ways. Most people like to receive a gift: we look forward to opening it and discovering what has been given in love. I know from my own family that children cannot wait to open a present. Before Christmas Day I have caught my children shaking the wrapped presents, and even peeling back the paper to peep at what is inside. When I was a young lad I had an older cousin who at Christmas would always buy the latest gadget for me. Others bought me socks and aftershave, but he would always buy something exciting. His was always the first present I wanted to open!

As God's people we need to understand that the Lord loves His people, and wants us to move forward in His purposes for our lives. He loves to bring insight that will help us grow closer to Him. His delight is to bring us, by His Holy Spirit, the gift of wisdom. For many traditional Christians today, the action of the Holy Spirit within a believer's life is untaught and unknown. Many churches do not teach of the work that the Holy Spirit wants to do in the lives of those who follow Jesus. But one of the simplest truths that Jesus came to bring to us was that through faith in Him we become children of a personal heavenly Father! In the Old Testament, God is rarely referred to as "Father," but through Jesus the love of God's fatherly heart is made clear to all of us. Often God is described as "Father," by Jesus and by the early disciples – meaning those who have put their trust in Jesus. As our heavenly Father, it is God's desire that through His Holy Spirit we might be assured of all that He has given us as His children. As children of God we have been given the Holy Spirit as a guide to lead us into truth. One of the true signs that someone is a child of God is that they are led by the Spirit. In Romans 8:14–15 we read:

> ... because those who are led by the Spirit of God are sons of God. For you did not receive a spirit that makes you a slave again to fear, but you received the Spirit of sonship. And by him we cry, *"Abba,* Father."

Here at the heart of Christian salvation is this wonderful truth of our identity in Christ! When we repent of our sins and give our lives to Jesus, we receive from God His Spirit, who moves us into a Father–child relationship with God Himself. Heaven is set apart for the children of God, a place where those adopted into the family of God by faith in Jesus will live. We cannot enter the Kingdom of God unless we are born again, because by being born again we receive the Spirit of sonship – which makes God our own Father and us His own children! By being born again we become alive spiritually to the Father as He sends the spirit of adoption into our hearts. This is why Paul declares in Romans 8:15–16:

> ... by him we cry, *"Abba,* Father." The Spirit himself testifies with our spirit that we are God's children.

This is not a manipulation of our need for a father who never lets us down. This is a spiritual work of God to bring us into His family, through faith in Jesus. Once we had the spirit of this world in our hearts and minds, which led us into sin, judgment and death. But now we have been given the spirit of liberty and life, the spirit of wisdom and power, because the Spirit of God Himself comes and lives in us to create confidence that we belong to Him. Look at Romans 8:14: "those who are led by the Spirit of God are sons of God." And 2 Corinthians 6:17–18 also describes this transformation into children of God:

> "Touch no unclean thing,
> and I will receive you."
> "I will be a Father to you,
> and you will be my sons and daughters,
> says the Lord Almighty."

The Lord gives us an inner witness of our adoption as His children. He does this so that we might be confident in the great love He has lavished on us as His children. 1 John 3:1–2 declares that this relationship has been given because of God's love for us:

> How great is the love the Father has *lavished* on us, that we should be called *children of God*! And that is what we are! The reason the world does not know us is that it did not know him. Dear friends, now we are children of God . . .
>
> (emphasis added)

As God's children we should allow the Holy Spirit to lead us into rejoicing and gladness, because we have a Father in heaven. We have a family that transcends the grave. This is why the promises of God are so important to us: these promises are not just given to anyone, but only to us as children of the eternal Father, who empowers and equips His children to live lives pleasing to Him. We come from Him, we have been given life by Him, so He releases good gifts to us as His children. One of those gifts is wisdom:

> Every good and perfect gift is from above, coming down from the Father of the heavenly lights ... He chose to give us birth through the word of truth, that we might be a kind of firstfruits of all he created.
>
> (James 1:17–18)

As children of the living God we should all understand what a wonderful companion the Holy Spirit is to those who open their hearts and minds to Him. In the last chapter we saw how pathways of wisdom are created in our minds by reading and meditating on Scripture. And this process is deepened by the powerful work of the Holy Spirit, to become personal and heartfelt revelation.

One of the joys of being a pastor is to see many Christians open their hearts to the baptism of the Holy Spirit that Jesus promised to those who love Him. Without exception, I have seen these folk come to a deeper awareness of their salvation. They have understood the depth of God's love for them in Jesus' taking their sin, guilt and punishment, and dying in their place on the cross. Ideas they heard many times before have become, in a matter of weeks, fountains of life, confidence and release. Through the Holy Spirit's prompting they have been led to a personal, sincere response. I have seen Christians who for years have been stunted in their growth, when they receive the Holy Spirit, suddenly released into freedom and wisdom. They can now live out the decrees of Scripture and see the truth of God's promises released into their lives. All this has happened because the Holy Spirit has become their teacher, shedding light on the Lord's written Word.

The Lord Jesus wants us to grow into the knowledge of heavenly wisdom. By the Holy Spirit's teaching this wisdom bears good fruit in our lives, enabling us to enjoy the blessings of Kingdom living. When we put Galatians 5 alongside James 3 we see how both the fruit and the wisdom of the Spirit work together in the life of believers.

Let us compare these verses:

> But the fruit of the Spirit is love, joy, peace, patience, kindness, goodness, faithfulness, gentleness and self-control.
>
> (Galatians 5:22–23)

> But the wisdom that comes from heaven is first of all pure; then peace-loving, considerate, submissive, full of mercy and good fruit, impartial and sincere.
>
> (James 3:17)

The Holy Spirit, through our hearts and minds, equips the children of God to grow into the nature of Jesus. If we put aside our fear and skepticism of the Holy Spirit and allow the Word to lead our responses to Him, then we can receive heavenly wisdom that will even confound Satan and the forces of evil around us. In 1 Corinthians 2:7–8 we read:

> No, we speak of God's secret wisdom, a wisdom that has been hidden and that God destined for our glory before time began. None of the rulers of this age understood it, for if they had, they would not have crucified the Lord of glory.

It is a simple truth that we have been saved through the sacrifice of Jesus on the cross. When Satan conspired for Jesus to be crucified, he was so blinded by the desire for revenge and victory that he did not see he was actually implementing the very plan of God Himself to save humanity. How Satan must have wailed when Jesus rose from the dead and snatched the keys of hell! How he must have wailed when Jesus ascended to the right hand of the Father! How he must have wailed when he realized that Jesus is the Lamb of God who has taken away the sin of the whole world, and opened up a new and living way to the Father through His blood. Blinded by his hatred of all that belonged to the Lord, Satan was surprised by the salvation plan of God. If Satan himself cannot understand the mind of God, nor by sinful knowledge reason out the plans of the Lord, how can we use worldly understanding to reason the plans of God?

With the Holy Spirit as teacher, there is wonderful joy. Here is the amazing promise of God that brings freedom and hope into our lives. What we cannot grasp by human knowledge, nor obtain by the world's understanding, we have been freely given by the Holy Spirit of God. The Holy Spirit comes into our lives to help us understand the means of our salvation, to enable us to live lives worthy of Christ, and to guide us in the will of God.

Throughout Scripture we see that when the Holy Spirit came upon people they were given insights by God. They prophesied, saw visions, and were given wisdom to make decisions in line with the Lord's will. Romans 12 and 1 Corinthians 12 describe many practical and spiritual gifts given to the Lord's people, as together we seek to serve Him and fulfill His mission here on earth. These include gifts of revelation to lead and educate God's people; and gifts such as prophecy, teaching, leadership, administration, the speaking of wisdom or words of knowledge, discerning between spirits, interpretation of tongues – all given by the same Spirit for the building up of God's people.

How can we doubt the activity of the Lord to guide His church, when so many of the gifts He wants to pour out on to us bring revelation of His will? Scripture makes it clear that the church has its existence in Jesus. He is the head of the church, so that His thoughts and ways might govern its actions. This is why the Holy Spirit is released over His people to guide us. If we do not learn to be sensitive to the Holy Spirit, and take time to listen to His direction, then even as the body of the Lord Jesus we are building on a shaky foundation. In the everyday direction of our lives and our churches, we need the wisdom of the Holy Spirit.

Jesus Himself was led by the Holy Spirit. He listened and responded to what the Holy Spirit said to Him. Matthew 4:1

tells us: "Then Jesus was led by the Spirit into the desert to be tempted by the devil." The word for "led" here means "brought" or "launched," which shows that the Holy Spirit revealed a course of action to Jesus, and He responded in obedience to the Spirit's guidance. The teaching that Jesus gave to His disciples was also directed by the Holy Spirit within Him. In Acts 1:1–2 we see that the wisdom of Jesus was given through the Holy Spirit:

> ...I wrote about all that Jesus began to do and to teach, until the day he was taken up to heaven, after giving instructions through the Holy Spirit to the apostles He had chosen.

No wonder Jesus tells us we need not worry about what to say when we are taken before the courts of the land, for the Holy Spirit will teach us how to bear witness to Him.

The Book of Acts shows that it was the Holy Spirit who gave direction to the early church. He made opportunities for ministry, provided wisdom for the use of resources, gave words to testify, and explained what was to come. It was the Holy Spirit who enabled wise decisions to be made, enabling the early church to grow powerfully. The church grew not just through signs and wonders, but by godly wisdom released by the Spirit of the Lord. Jesus declares even today: "I will build my church, and the gates of Hades will not overcome it" (Matthew 16:18).

There should be within all of us, as God's people, hearts that respond to the guidance and prompting of the Holy Spirit. At the center of God's will for our lives, we find His promises made real. We should not be frightened of the spiritual expression of our faith, but on the foundation of Scripture we should respond continuously to the gift of the Spirit. Knowledge of the Word on its own will only puff a person up with pride, unless the Holy Spirit is our teacher. Knowledge without the fruit of godly wisdom, without the fruit of the Holy Spirit, becomes self-seeking: a badge of honor rather than a fountain of

life. The Lord has created our minds and enabled our understanding, so we can apply intellect alone to the study of God.
But the human intellect is fallen, and therefore its concepts and
theologies are fallen. This is true of all we conceive, if it is by the
mind alone that we approach the Lord and His ways. I know
many people who have completed a theological degree at
university, and yet are confused and ignorant about the
purposes of the living God. We must be open and responsive
to a heavenly wisdom taught by the greatest teacher of all:
the Lord God.

Chapter 10

TESTING *and*
AFFIRMING
GOD'S PLANS

Trust in the LORD with all your heart
and lean not on your own understanding;
in all your ways acknowledge him,
and he will make your paths straight.
(Proverbs 3:5–6)

I wonder how good you are at understanding signposts? As part of the driving test, we have to recognize signs and explain what they mean. Some are more useful than others. In this book we have considered how to cultivate our minds to enable us to live lives worthy of Jesus, and to follow His plan for our lives. We have examined how our society shapes our thinking, often trapping our minds in worldly patterns that are not helpful to our relationship with the Lord. In the light of this we have explored how God can transform the way we think by the renewing of our minds, so that our understanding is centered on the wisdom of His Kingdom. We have seen how the renewal of our minds takes us from a worldly viewpoint, beyond the temporary foolishness of man's wisdom, to be set free to grow in the mind of Christ. The final stage of growth is discovering the plans the Lord has for every individual. The

Word of God tells us that the Lord has a specific plan for each one of us. This plan is not only for now, but also for the future.

One of the wonderful truths about our lives in Jesus is that each of us is called to fulfill the purposes of God, and the plans He has made for our lives are secure. Psalm 33:10–11 tells us:

> The LORD foils the plans of the nations;
>> he thwarts the purposes of the peoples.
> But the plans of the LORD stand firm forever,
>> the purposes of his heart through all generations.

If we put theses verses alongside Jeremiah 29:11, this is the message we are given:

God has a specific plan for your life that will prosper you and give you a future, and these plans made in the heart of God for your life stand forever! Nothing will thwart God's good and perfect plan for you as you walk in obedience and trust.

We therefore need to consider as God's people how to discover His will for our lives. We all come to crossroads in our lives: times when we have to make decisions, and need the direction and wisdom of the Lord Jesus. How do we discover this wisdom?

One of the first things that Scripture tells us is to commit our circumstances, decisions and relationships to the Lord. We are promised in the Bible that if we bring Jesus into our lives right at the start of the decision-making process, He will direct our paths. Proverbs 3:5–6 calls us not to see things through the eyes of our own understanding, but to trust the Lord. If we seek His perfect will, we shall receive it:

> Trust in the LORD with all your heart
>> and lean not on your own understanding;
> in all your ways acknowledge him,
>> and he will make your paths straight.

Faith in God is the fundamental characteristic that God is looking for in us, His people, *if* we want Him to bless us in our daily lives! We cannot have peace, joy or hope in our lives if we do not fully trust in Jesus and His salvation. The Lord seeks those who have absolute trust in Him, and we all need to cultivate a deeper trust in Him. If we don't build our trust in the Lord now, no security in our life will survive when the difficult times come. We all know the story in Genesis 41, where Joseph is taken before the Pharaoh of Egypt because the Pharaoh has had a dream. The meaning of the dream is that there will be seven years of prosperity followed by seven years of famine. There is a spiritual principle in the story. Joseph gives the Pharaoh this advice:

> Let Pharaoh appoint commissioners over the land to take a fifth of the harvest of Egypt during the seven years of abundance. They should collect all the food of these good years that are coming and store up the grain ... This food should be held in reserve for the country, to be used during the seven years of famine ...
>
> (Genesis 41:34–36)

The principle is that each one of us needs to cultivate our trust in God *now*. We need to enter into His promises, learn from His Word, and excise from our lives anything that causes us to doubt His goodness. If we do this now, we will be ready when the hard times come in our lives.

Trust is something that we cultivate, as we immerse ourselves in the things of God. The Spirit of God cannot guide us unless we trust in Him to guide our footsteps. This is why trust in God is the first quality to cultivate, in order to let go of our own understanding and follow His direction for our lives. Like Joseph, we need God's wisdom to increase our reserves of trust now, so that we will have all we need for times of famine in the future.

As God's people we must be rooted and grounded in Jesus.

We need to work hard at deepening our reserves of trust in Him. Promises are given to those who cultivate hearts that trust in the Lord. These promises are a resource enabling us to let go of ourselves, to allow the Lord to guide us through the important decisions in our lives. If we trust in the Lord, His promise is that He will never leave us or forsake us. Whether we go through good or bad times, He will be by our side. Psalm 9:9–10 tells us:

> The LORD is a refuge for the oppressed,
>   a stronghold in times of trouble.
> Those who know your name will trust in you,
>   for you, LORD have *never* forsaken those who seek you.
>
>   (emphasis added)

This is the testimony of those who follow the Lord. He will not forsake those who trust in Him, so we must not be afraid to allow Him to direct our lives. Even when an episode is not finished in our lives, He will continue it until it is completed, for those who trust Him.

If we trust in God we find rest for our souls, because He is the one who secures us in salvation and holds our destiny in His hands. Psalm 62:5–8 says:

> Find rest, O my soul, in God alone;
>   my hope comes from him.
> He alone is my rock and my salvation;
>   he is my fortress, I shall not be shaken.
> My salvation and my honor depend on God;
>   he is my mighty rock, my refuge.
> *Trust in him at all times, O people* . . .
>
>   (emphasis added)

The Holy Spirit seeks to use the trust we have in Jesus to bless us with the fruit of the Spirit. Joy, peace and hope are dependent on our deep trust in God:

> May the God of hope fill you with all joy and peace as you
> trust in him, so that you may overflow with hope by the
> power of the Holy Spirit.
>
> (Romans 15:13)

The Lord's love abides in us when we trust in Him. Trust
means that we understand who the Lord is, and acknowledge in
our hearts and minds the goodness of His character. We know
that the Lord is good, that His love endures forever, that He is
faithful to His people and that He will not let our feet slip.
When we like children simply entrust our lives to Him, we are
declaring: "Yes Lord, you are totally trustworthy in all Your
ways." When we put this conviction into practice as a sign of
obedience, the Lord pours out His love on our lives. Psalm
32:10 tells us:

> Many are the woes of the wicked,
>   but the LORD's unfailing love
>   surrounds the man who trusts in him.

The love of the Lord is expressed in His promise of prosperity
to those who trust and obey Him. This is not prosperity as
sinful man would define it, but prosperity in the things of the
Kingdom. It will cause our lives to grow in Him, as we establish
His will in our lives:

> A greedy man stirs up dissension,
>   but he who trusts in the LORD will prosper.
>
> (Proverbs 28:25)

The Lord promises to secure our lives in Him and to keep safe
what we entrust to Him, even our very lives. Here is the
wonderful truth: we can cast our burdens on the Lord because
He cares for us. We can commit ourselves to Him because He
holds us in the palm of His hand. Proverbs 29:25 gives us this
great encouragement:

> Fear of man will prove to be a snare,
>> but whoever trusts in the LORD is kept safe.

If we learn to trust in God as a good Father who helps His children, then He will help us whenever we call on Him in our time of need. We need to cultivate this trust in the good times, so that in the bad times our natural response is to call upon His name:

> Praise be to the LORD,
>> for he has heard my cry for mercy.
> The LORD is my strength and my shield;
>> my heart trusts in him, and I am helped.

> (Psalm 28:6–7)

The Lord empowers and strengthens us to ensure that what He has promised is fulfilled in our lives. When we make our own plans, we have no guarantee of help; but when we listen to the Lord and walk down the path He directs, He enables us to succeed and not give up. By His Holy Spirit the Lord renews our strength at times of tiredness, so that we can continue being faithful and obedient to Him. In Isaiah 40:30–31, renewal of strength is promised if we put our hope in the Lord:

> Even youths grow tired and weary,
>> and young men stumble and fall;
> but those who hope in the LORD
>> will renew their strength.
> They will soar on wings like eagles;
>> they will run and not grow weary,
>> they will walk and not be faint.

God's promises challenge us to let go of our own plans and commit our ways to the Lord. These promises from the Word of God are biblical reasons why we need to cultivate our trust in the Lord Jesus.

To see the perfect will of God operate in our lives, we need to place every situation into His hands and allow His perfect will to take control as our lives are worked out. The problem is that we make token gestures in prayer to commit our ways to the Lord, but deep down we have our minds set on a certain outcome. God has a plan for our lives that will not pass away. If we truly belong to Him He will give to us, and take from us, so that His perfect will is made manifest in our lives. We need godly wisdom: at the start of each venture we must give the Lord complete freedom and authority to govern the outcome, so that His perfect will is fulfilled in our lives. It is hard for us as Christians to live in such radical obedience, but this is God's prescribed way of directing His people.

What we are considering is a simple matter of trust. Can we trust the Lord to do what is best for us? Can we trust Him to guide our lives as we seek His purposes for us, His people? Whenever we trust someone's advice, we assess the character of the person to know whether they are trustworthy. We are sure that the Lord is perfectly trustworthy in all His ways. He is completely faithful to His people. When He gives His word, He means it. When He makes a promise, He always keeps it. Perfect love, perfect justice, perfect goodness are in God and come from God. He is the Lord who does not change. He is not swayed by the shifting demands of man, and the authority of His Word does not vary. He can always be trusted to do what is right for His people. Therefore it makes perfect sense for us to seek and accept what the Lord has prescribed for us. Committing our ways to Him is a natural response to the wonderful Savior and Lord whom we know as God.

Having committed our lives into the hands of God, we need to push some doors to see where He is leading us. I have often seen Christians stagnate because they will not make a decision in their lives, in case they "get it wrong." They are frightened of mis-hearing, so they are frightened of stepping out in faith. But if we commit our ways to the Lord, there is no right or wrong: only a clarifying of the Lord's will. Whenever we push a door, it will either open or stay shut. When we have handed over our future to the Lord and His sovereign hand is on our situation, even a closed door leads us nearer to the open door of a God-given opportunity. We know that the Lord uses angels to speak to His people. He uses dreams, prophecies and visions to reveal His will for our lives. He also uses the opening of "doors" to confirm a course of action. If you have no sense of direction in a certain area of your life, then commit the situation to God, push the doors, and see what happens. If nothing comes immediately then push doors more widely until you have a sense of direction and purpose. The Lord does not try to make things difficult for us, or trick us. He wants us to know His purposes and follow His plan for our lives. God's timing is always perfect, and we need to be open to His timing. If we follow these precepts, He will guide us even in our times of waiting.

In every situation there are two doors that we can go through: the door of our own ambition and desire, or the door of God's ordained will and opportunity. Revelation 3:7–8 teaches us:

> These are the words of him who is holy and true, who holds the key of David. What he opens no-one can shut, and what he shuts no-one can open. I know your deeds. See, I have placed before you an open door that no-one can shut.

It is the Lord's desire that we walk through the open door of His purpose. Can you see here the grace and goodness of Jesus? He knows our deeds and our needs, and He has opened the door to divinely-appointed plans for our lives. We should not sit back and wait to see what happens, but rather push those doors of opportunity, and test whether they are open or closed to us. As we faithfully seek the Lord's will in small things, He opens up the doors to bigger appointments. Do not let fear bind you, make you stop or stagnate, for the Lord will not let you open a door which is closed to you by His will. If we push many doors, God will lead us through His chosen, open door of opportunity.

As we try to discern God's plan and make right decisions, we can *put out fleeces* to affirm God's will for our lives. I know some people frown on "fleecing," seeing in it a lack of faith, but if the intention is to affirm the Lord's will and not to test Him, then fleecing is acceptable to God. Putting out fleeces is not about testing God or seeking a manifestation of the supernatural: it is done recognizing that any of us can "get it wrong," but that we are passionate about being in God's will and so we are asking Him to confirm a plan.

The idea of fleecing comes from Gideon, who looked to discern that God was with Him and affirming his course of action:

> Gideon said to God, "If you will save Israel by my hand as you have promised – look, I will place a wool fleece on the threshing-floor. If there is dew only on the fleece and all the ground is dry, then I will know that you will save Israel by my hand, as you said." And that is what happened. Gideon rose early the next day; he squeezed the fleece and wrung out the dew – a bowlful of water.
>
> (Judges 6:36–38)

Perhaps at this moment, in some area of your life, you need to put a fleece out to clarify a course of action. I have myself "fleeced" to confirm what the Lord was saying to me. Once, I felt strongly within myself that the Lord was calling me to Bible college. I was not particularly academic, and had a very active ministry at the time. So I said to the Lord: "Lord, I'm going to this college for a celebration weekend. If you want me to stay there for a year, send me a student or lecturer to tell me that you want me at the college." I went to the celebration weekend as I had planned, and had a really good time. The worship was powerful, the Word solid, and the fellowship warm and encouraging. Meeting after meeting went by, and I just relaxed in the Lord and His love.

Then, at the end of one late-night celebration, a young lady walked up to me. I did not know her, so I looked around expecting to see someone waving at her. But she came right up to me, and said simply: "As I was in worship at the start of the meeting, the Lord told me to come up to you and say that He wants you at this college." I listened to what she said, and as I looked down at her jacket I saw a badge saying "Cliff College Student." I never saw her again, but my prayer had been specifically answered. A student of the college had come to me and told me the Lord wanted me there!

There are different ways of "putting out fleeces," but the intention should always be to affirm and clarify the will of the Lord for our lives. God does not want us to guess at His chosen direction for us. He has placed His Holy Spirit within us so that we might be renewed through His plans for us. He is willing to clarify His direction with signs, to calm our fears and strengthen our obedience to Him.

Along with this, the Lord makes His plans clear to us through the guidance of our spiritual brothers and sisters. As Christians we have been brought into a body of believers who are responsible for our lives, as we are responsible for theirs. Throughout the life of the early church, the callings and ministries of individuals were tested by those who were more mature in faith. As people of God we see how the Lord shapes the lives of the brothers and sisters around us. He is completely consistent in the ways He works through our lives. Whatever the Lord calls us to, He also equips us and shapes us for. We can go to mature, discerning brothers and sisters in the church with the concerns of our hearts and minds, and seek God's wisdom through the ministry of each other in the body of Christ. Acts 13:2–3 gives an example of this:

> While they were worshiping the Lord and fasting, the Holy Spirit said, "Set apart for me Barnabas and Saul for the work to which I have called them." So after they had fasted and prayed, they placed their hands on them and sent them off.

The leaders were open to the guidance and revelation that came through the body of Christ by the Holy Spirit. When we are on the verge of making an important decision we need to go to a wise brother or sister in the church, seeking their prayer and counsel. This is God's chosen way to affirm His direction for our lives. We need to lay aside our fears and put away double-mindedness. We need to trust that the Lord Jesus' plan for us is perfect and will secure our future in Him. His plan never passes away, and He has given us biblical processes to follow that open up His will for our lives. As the Spirit brings the deep things of God into our lives and creates within us the mind of Christ, great new horizons are made possible for us all. As we allow the Holy Spirit to dwell within us, to richly deepen our passion for Jesus, then His thoughts, His ways, His plans are made available to us.

It is never too late to commit ourselves to God-given procedures to renew our lives. It does not matter how young or old we are in the faith, or how long we have been in the world, even as Christians. He is looking for each one of us to surrender heart and will, and say yes to His plans for us. He is looking for us to present ourselves as living sacrifices, willing to be transformed by the renewing of our minds, testing and affirming His perfect and pleasing will for us. Let me encourage each of you to ask now for this wisdom that comes from on high, and to cultivate it – for wisdom that renews our minds is a glorious gift from God to us, His precious children.

Appendix

BIBLE REFERENCES
on WISDOM *and* GOD'S PLANS

Old Testament

God is not a man, that he should lie,
    nor a son of man, that he should change his mind.

(Numbers 23:19)

Now Joshua son of Nun was filled with the spirit of wisdom because Moses had laid his hands on him. So the Israelites listened to him and did what the LORD had commanded Moses.

(Deuteronomy 34:9)

"I will raise up for myself a faithful priest, who will do according to what is in my heart and mind. I will firmly establish his house, and he will minister before my anointed one always."

(1 Samuel 2:35)

He who is the Glory of Israel does not lie or change his mind; for he is not a man, that he should change his mind.

(1 Samuel 15:29)

I will do what you have asked. I will give you a wise and discerning heart . . .

(1 Kings 3:12)

When all Israel heard the verdict the king had given, they held the king in awe, because they saw that he had wisdom from God to administer justice.

(1 Kings 3:28)

God gave Solomon wisdom and very great insight, and a breadth of understanding as measureless as the sand on the seashore.

(1 Kings 4:29)

The LORD gave Solomon wisdom, just as he had promised him.

(1 Kings 5:12)

The whole world sought audience with Solomon to hear the wisdom God had put in his heart.

(1 Kings 10:24)

"And you, my son Solomon, acknowledge the God of your father, and serve him with wholehearted devotion and with a willing mind, for the LORD searches every heart and understands every motive behind the thoughts."

(1 Chronicles 28:9)

"Give me wisdom and knowledge, that I may lead this people, for who is able to govern this great people of yours?"
   ". . . therefore wisdom and knowledge will be given you."

(2 Chronicles 1:10, 12)

He thwarts the plans of the crafty,
   so that their hands achieve no success.

(Job 5:12)

"To God belong wisdom and power;
  counsel and understanding are his."

(Job 12:13)

"And he said to man,
  'The fear of the LORD – that is wisdom,
  and to shun evil is understanding.' "

(Job 28:28)

"Who endowed the heart with wisdom
  or gave understanding to the mind?"

(Job 38:36)

The law of the LORD is perfect,
  reviving the soul.
The statutes of the LORD are trustworthy,
  making wise the simple.
The precepts of the LORD are right,
  giving joy to the heart.
The commands of the LORD are radiant,
  giving light to the eyes.

(Psalm 19:7–8)

The LORD foils the plans of the nations;
  he thwarts the purposes of the peoples.
But the plans of the LORD stand firm for ever,
  the purposes of his heart through all
    generations.

(Psalm 33:10–11)

The mouth of the righteous man utters wisdom,
  and his tongue speaks what is just.
The law of his God is in his heart;
  his feet do not slip.

(Psalm 37:30–31)

They plot injustice and say,
  "We have devised a perfect plan!"
Surely the mind and heart of man are cunning.

(Psalm 64:6)

The fear of the LORD is the beginning of wisdom;
  all who follow his precepts have good understanding.
To him belongs eternal praise.

(Psalm 111:10)

The fear of the LORD is the beginning of knowledge,
  but fools despise wisdom and discipline.

(Proverbs 1:7)

turning your ear to wisdom
  and applying your heart to understanding,
and if you call out for insight
  and cry aloud for understanding,
and if you look for it as for silver
  and search for it as for hidden treasure,
then you will understand the fear of the LORD
  and find the knowledge of God.
For the LORD gives wisdom,
  and from his mouth come knowledge and understanding.

(Proverbs 2:2–6)

"The fear of the LORD is the beginning of wisdom,
  and knowledge of the Holy One is understanding.
For through me your days will be many,
  and years will be added to your life.
If you are wise, your wisdom will reward you..."

(Proverbs 9:10–12)

The fear of the LORD teaches a man wisdom...

(Proverbs 15:33)

Commit to the LORD whatever you do,
and your plans will succeed.

(Proverbs 16:3)

In his heart a man plans his course,
but the LORD determines his steps.

(Proverbs 16:9)

Many are the plans in a man's heart,
but it is the LORD's purpose that prevails.

(Proverbs 19:21)

To the man who pleases him, God gives wisdom, knowledge
and happiness . . .

(Ecclesiastes 2:26)

So I turned my mind to understand,
to investigate and to search out wisdom and
the scheme of things
and to understand the stupidity of wickedness
and the madness of folly.

(Ecclesiastes 7:25)

The Spirit of the LORD will rest on him –
the Spirit of wisdom and of understanding,
the Spirit of counsel and of power,
the Spirit of knowledge and of the fear of the LORD –
and he will delight in the fear of the LORD.

(Isaiah 11:2–3)

You will keep in perfect peace
him whose mind is steadfast,
because he trusts in you.
Trust in the LORD for ever,
for the LORD, the LORD, is the Rock eternal.

(Isaiah 26:3–4)

"Woe to the obstinate children,"
     declares the LORD,
"to those who carry out plans that are not mine ... "

                                        (Isaiah 30:1)

He will be the sure foundation for your times,
     a rich store of salvation and wisdom and knowledge;
the fear of the LORD is the key to this treasure.

                                        (Isaiah 33:6)

Who has understood the Spirit of the LORD,
     or instructed him as his counsellor?
Whom did the LORD consult to enlighten him,
     and who taught him the right way?
Who was it that taught him knowledge
     or showed him the path of understanding?

                                        (Isaiah 40:13–14)

But, O LORD Almighty, you who judge righteously
     and test the heart and mind ...

                                        (Jeremiah 11:20)

"I the LORD search the heart
     and examine the mind,
to reward a man according to his conduct,
     according to what his deeds deserve."

                                        (Jeremiah 17:10)

O LORD Almighty, you who examine the righteous
     and probe the heart and mind ...

                                        (Jeremiah 20:12)

"For I know the plans I have for you," declares the LORD,
"plans to prosper you and not to harm you, plans to give you
hope and a future."

                                        (Jeremiah 29:11)

"This is the covenant that I will make
    with the house of Israel
after that time," declares the LORD.
"I will put my law in their minds
    and write it on their hearts.
I will be their God,
    and they will be my people."

(Jeremiah 31:33)

"Praise be to the name of God for ever and ever;
    wisdom and power are His.
He changes times and seasons;
    he sets up kings and deposes them.
He gives wisdom to the wise
    and knowledge to the discerning.
He reveals deep and hidden things . . .

(Daniel 2:20–22)

New Testament

The mind of sinful man is death, but the mind controlled by the Spirit is life and peace; the sinful mind is hostile to God. It does not submit to God's law, nor can it do so. Those controlled by the sinful nature cannot please God.

(Romans 8:6–8)

Do not conform any longer to the pattern of this world, but be transformed by the renewing of your mind. Then you will be able to test and approve what God's will is – his good, pleasing and perfect will.

(Romans 12:2)

See 1 Corinthians 1–2.

> "For who has known the mind of the Lord
> that he may instruct him?"

But we have the mind of Christ.

(1 Corinthians 2:16)

Do not deceive yourselves. If any one of you thinks he is wise by the standards of this age, he should become a "fool" so that he may become wise. For the wisdom of this world is foolishness in God's sight. As it is written; "He catches the wise in their craftiness"; and again, "The Lord knows that the thoughts of the wise are futile."

(1 Corinthians 3:18–20)

When I planned this, did I do it lightly? Or do I make my plans in a worldly manner so that in the same breath I say, "Yes, yes" and "No, no"?

(2 Corinthians 1:17)

The god of this age has blinded the minds of unbelievers, so that they cannot see the light of the gospel of the glory of Christ, who is the image of God.

(2 Corinthians 4:4)

So we fix our eyes not on what is seen, but on what is unseen. For what is seen is temporary, but what is unseen is eternal.

(2 Corinthians 4:18)

But I am afraid that just as Eve was deceived by the serpent's cunning, your minds may somehow be led astray from your sincere and pure devotion to Christ.

(2 Corinthians 11:3)

that the God of our Lord Jesus Christ, the Father of Glory, may give to you the spirit of wisdom and revelation in the knowledge of Him, the eyes of your understanding being enlightened; that you may know what is the hope of His calling, what are the riches of the glory of His inheritance in the saints, and what is the exceeding greatness of His power towards us who believe, according to the working of His mighty power.

(Ephesians 1:17–19 NKJV)

... that now the manifold wisdom of God might be made known by the church to the principalities and powers in the heavenly places.

(Ephesians 3:10 NKJV)

You were taught, with regard to your former way of life, to put off your old self, which is being corrupted by its deceitful desires; to be made new in the attitude of your minds; and to put on the new self, created to be like God in true righteousness and holiness.

(Ephesians 4:22–24)

Their destiny is destruction, their god is their stomach, and their glory is in their shame. Their mind is on earthly things.

(Philippians 3:19)

For this reason, since the day we heard about you, we have not stopped praying for you and asking God to fill you with the knowledge of his will through all spiritual wisdom and understanding. And we pray this in order that you may live a life worthy of the Lord and may please him in every way: bearing fruit in every good work, growing in the knowledge of God.

(Colossians 1:9–10)

Once you were alienated from God and were enemies in your minds because of your evil behavior.

(Colossians 1:21)

Since, then, you have been raised with Christ, set your hearts
on things above, where Christ is seated at the right hand of
God. Set your minds on things above, not on earthly things.

(Colossians 3:1–2)

...and have put on the new self, which is being renewed in
knowledge in the image of its Creator.

(Colossians 3:10)

...he saved us, not because of the righteous things we had
done, but because of his mercy. He saved us through the
washing of rebirth and renewal by the Holy Spirit.

(Titus 3:5)

Therefore, holy brothers, who share in the heavenly calling,
fix your thoughts on Jesus, the apostle and high priest whom
we confess.

(Hebrews 3:1)

"I will put my laws in their hearts,
    and I will write them on their minds."

(Hebrews 10:16)

Let us fix our eyes on Jesus, the author and perfecter of our
faith...

(Hebrews 12:2)

If any of you lacks wisdom, he should ask God, who gives
generously to all without finding fault, and it will be given to
him. But when he asks, he must believe and not doubt,
because he who doubts is like a wave of the sea, blown and
tossed by the wind. That man should not think he will receive
anything from the Lord; he is a double-minded man, unstable
in all he does.

(James 1:5–8)

But the wisdom that comes from heaven is first of all pure;
then peace-loving, considerate, submissive, full of mercy and
good fruit, impartial and sincere.

(James 3:17)

Therefore, prepare your minds for action; be self-controlled...

(1 Peter 1:13)

Then all the churches will know that I am he who searches
hearts and minds, and I will repay each of you according to
your deeds.

(Revelation 2:23)

We hope you enjoyed reading this Sovereign World book.
For more details of other Sovereign books
and new releases see our website:

www.sovereignworld.com

If you would like to help us send a copy of this book and
many other titles to needy pastors in developing countries,
please write for further information or send your gift to:

Sovereign World Trust
PO Box 777
Tonbridge, Kent TN11 0ZS
United Kingdom

You can also visit **www.sovereignworldtrust.com**.
The Trust is a registered charity.